Jarvis and Port Dover Ontario in Colour Photos, Saving Our History One Photo at a Time

Photography
by Barbara Raué
2014

Series Name:
Cruising Ontario

Book 67: Jarvis and Port Dover

Cover photo: Jones-Doughty Residence – one of the oldest homes in Jarvis, built in 1865 by local builders with the bricks supplied by the local Rodgers Brick Yard. Italianate style with dichromatic brickwork, arched voussoirs with keystones, paired cornice brackets, bay window on side

Series Name: Cruising Ontario
Saving Our History One Photo at a Time

Other Books by Barbara Raue

Coins of Gold

Arrows, Indians and Love

The Life and Times of Barbara
Volume 1: Inventions That Have Enhanced My Life
Volume 2: Entertainment That I Have Enjoyed
Volume 3: East Coast Trips
Volume 4: Olympics Have Always Intrigued Me
Volume 5: Wonders of the World
Volume 6: Caribbean Cruises We Have Enjoyed
Volume 7: Animals
Volume 8: Storms and Other Major Disasters in My Lifetime
Volume 9: Wars, Terrorist Attacks and Major Disasters

The Cromwell Family Book

Laura Secord Discovered

Visit Barbara's website to view all of her books
http://barbararaue.ca

Jarvis

Jarvis is located near the towns of Simcoe, Cayuga, Port Dover and Hagersville. Jarvis is strategically located at the junction of Highways 3 and 6. Jarvis has some excellent examples of brick architecture. Many of the historic homes were built after 1873. Many of the town's restaurants and shops are clustered around the intersection of the highways. The majority of the buildings are red brick.

Port Dover

In 1794, Mr. Peter Walker was the first settler of this community known as Dover Mills. During the War of 1812, there was an American raid here on May 14, 1814. After making their landing on the shore, 750 American soldiers launched a surprise attack on the village's civilians. Scattered elements of nearby militia and regular units tried to defend the village without any success. The survivors rebuilt Port Dover further downstream on Patterson's Creek on the north shore of Lake Erie. Port Dover is the southern terminus for Ontario Highway 6 located 480 kilometres or 300 miles to the south of the Northern Ontario community of McKerrow. This highway stretches northward as a two-lane, undivided highway until the traffic flow increases to four lanes shortly after it departs from Caledonia. This highway allows Port Dover residents direct access to the city of Hamilton, and on to Toronto.

The community once had its own railway station with frequent service from the Lake Erie & Northern Railway, owned by Canadian Pacific Railway. The Port Dover beaches caused most of the passenger traffic to occur during the summer months. A railway ticket to the "distant" community of Galt cost $1.55 per person during the late spring of 1949 (about $15.63 in today's money). Rail service was also offered on the Port Dover & Lake Huron Railway (later purchased by Canadian National) line from the Caledonia Train Station to Port Dover.

In 1974, the town was amalgamated into the new city of Nanticoke within the Regional Municipality of Haldimand-Norfolk.

The first Port Dover lighthouse was a twenty-four foot high wooden structure built on the west pier at the mouth of the Lynn River in 1845 as a small harbour light for the active shipbuilding, square timber trade, inshore fishery, and, later, coal and railway shipping.   It burned down in 1846 and was rebuilt in 1847.

Index

Jarvis

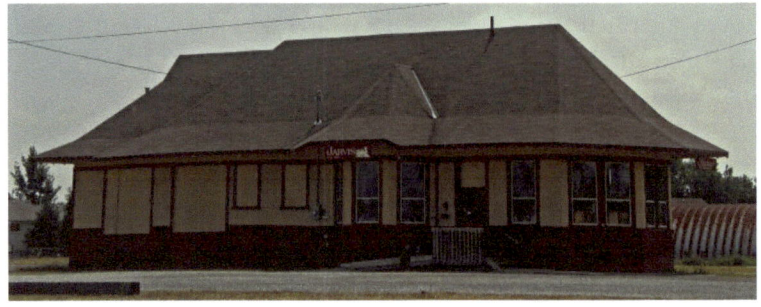

Jarvis Train Station

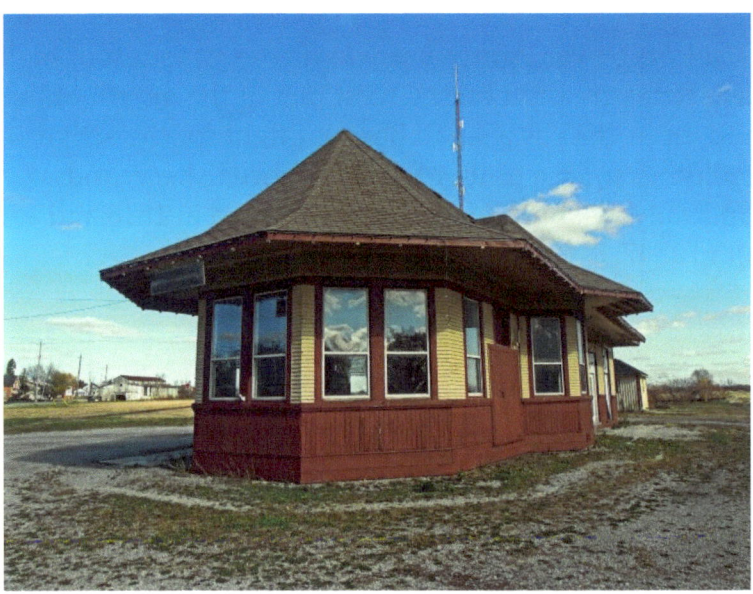

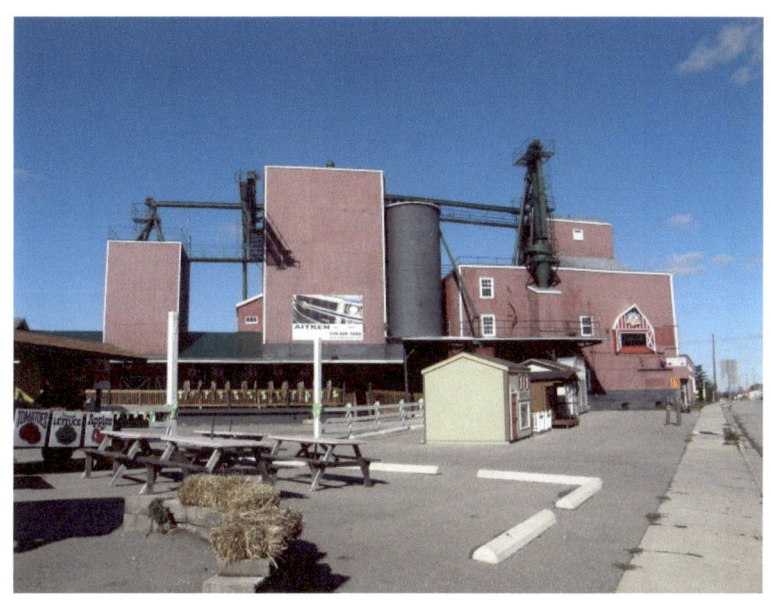

Grain elevators – now an antique market

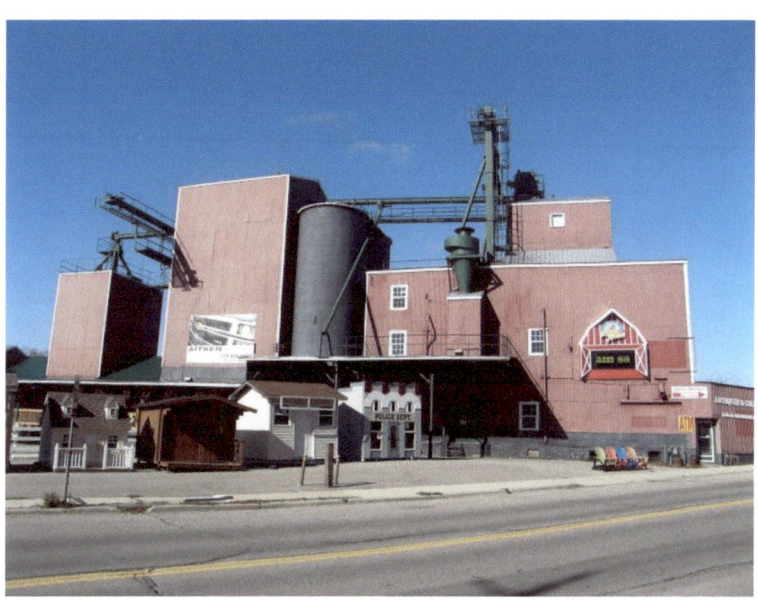

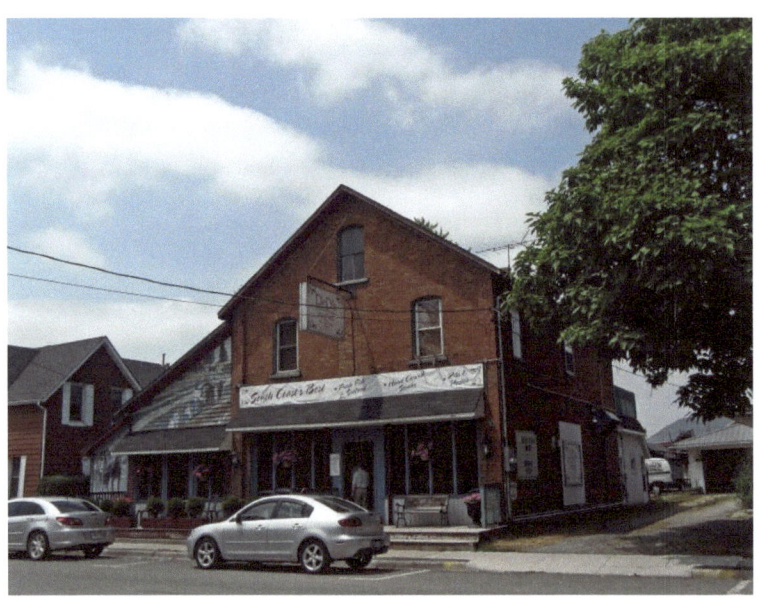

Dina D's Fine Family Dining – a great place for lunch – built in the 1880s

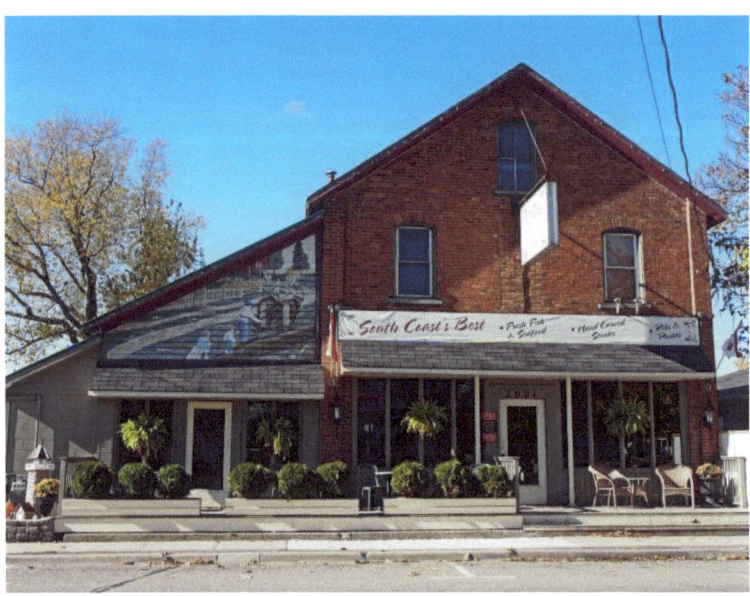

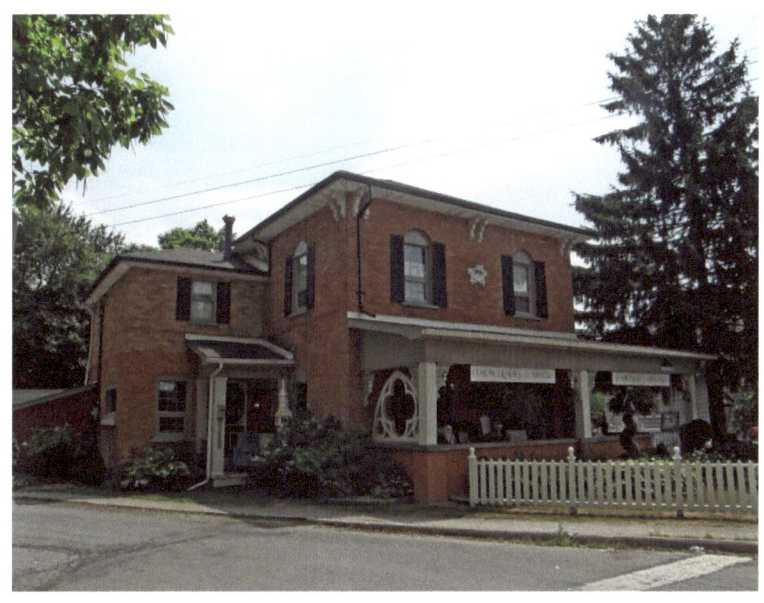

2092 Main Street – Italianate – c. 1870 - Italianate style

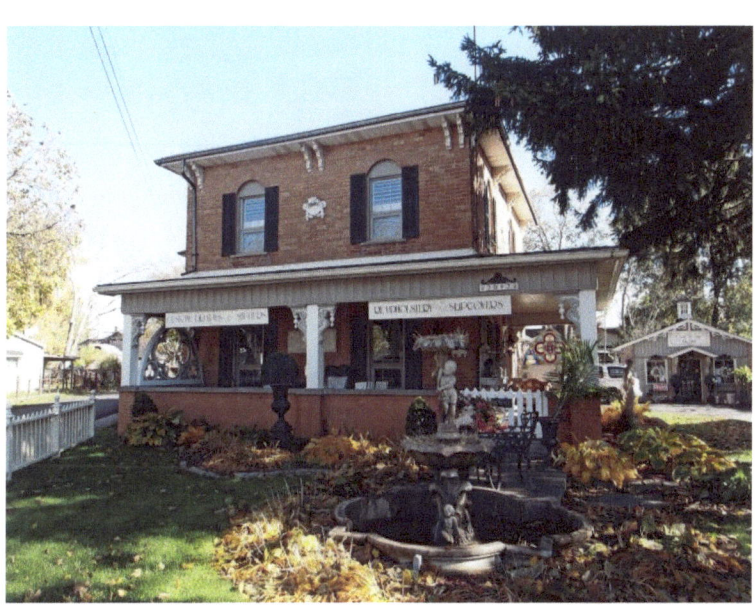

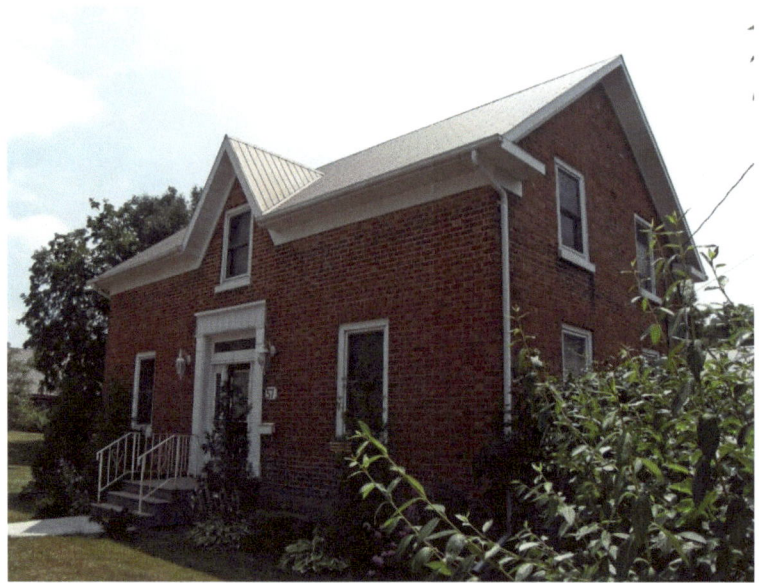

57 Talbot Street – 1½ storey Gothic Revival cottage, cornice return on end gable, red brick

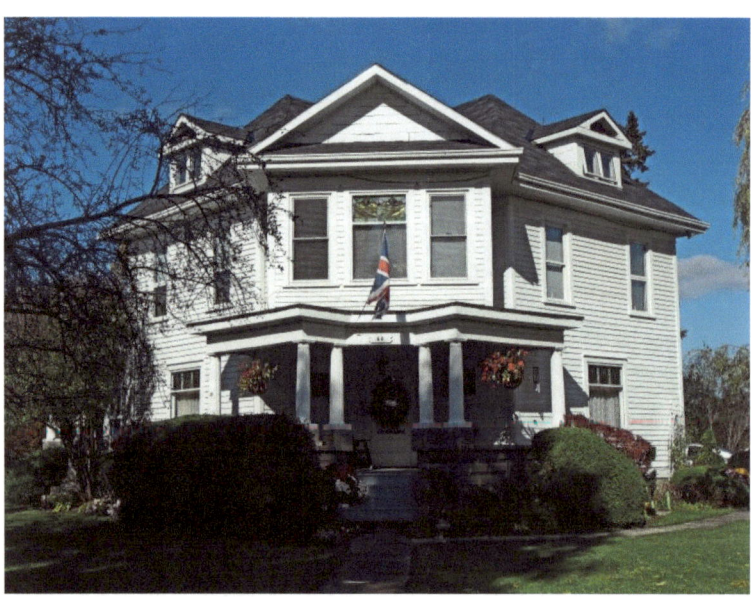

60 Talbot Street East – Italianate style with frontispiece, triangular pediment, dormer in the attic

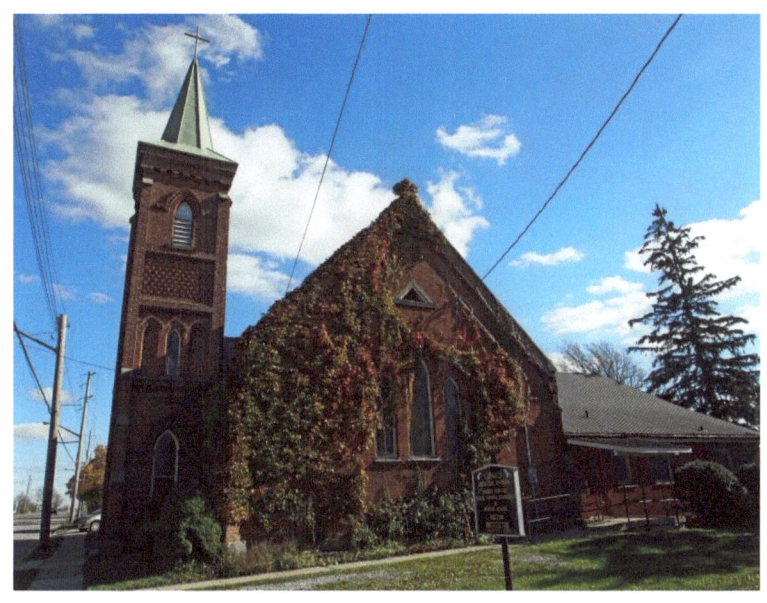

St. Paul's Anglican Church – 65 Talbot Street East

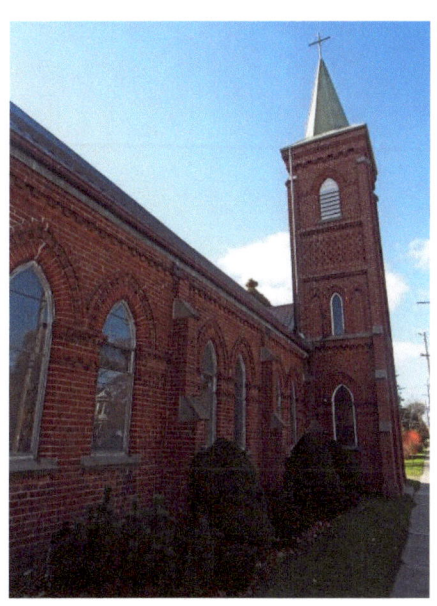

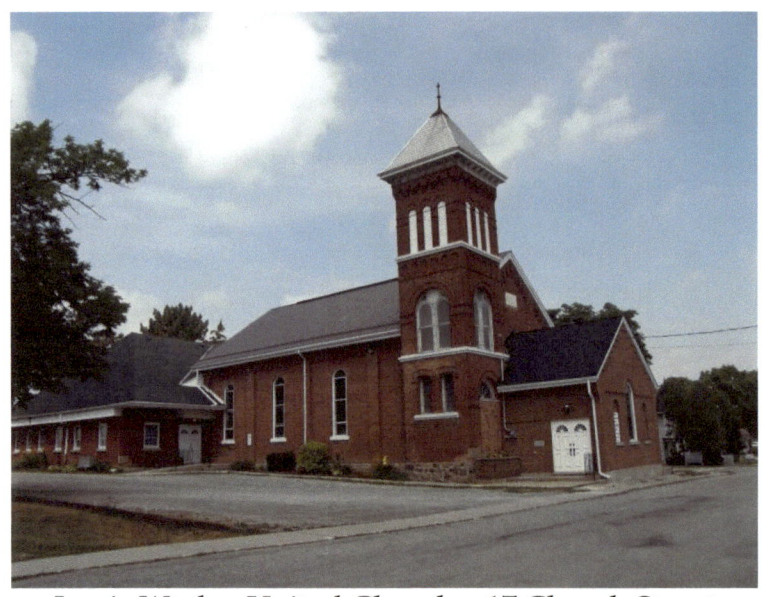

Jarvis Wesley United Church – 17 Church Street

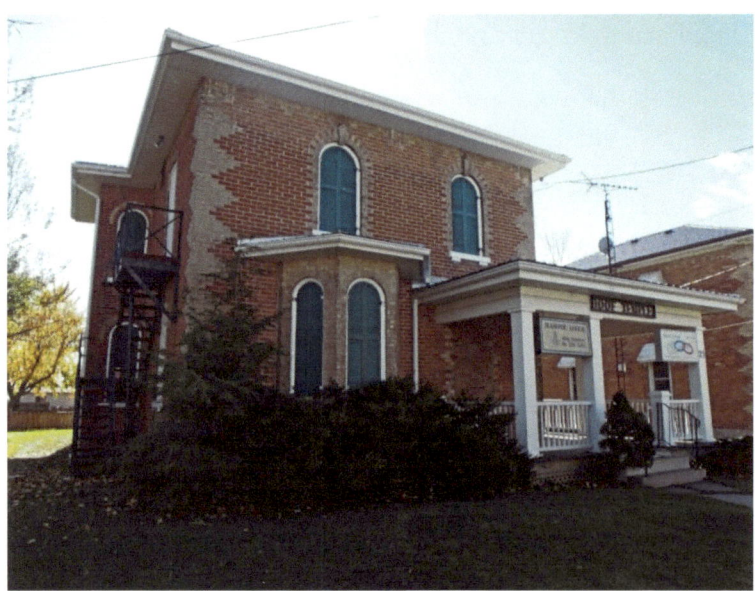

23 Talbot Street East – IOOF Temple – Masonic Lodge
Italianate style, dichromatic brickwork, bay window,
keystones above windows

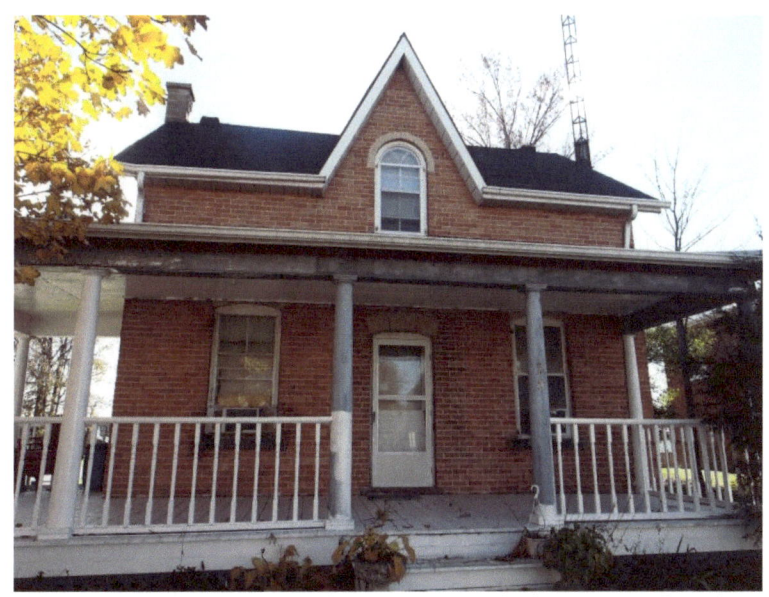

25 Talbot Street East – Gothic cottage, dichromatic brickwork, buff-coloured window hoods

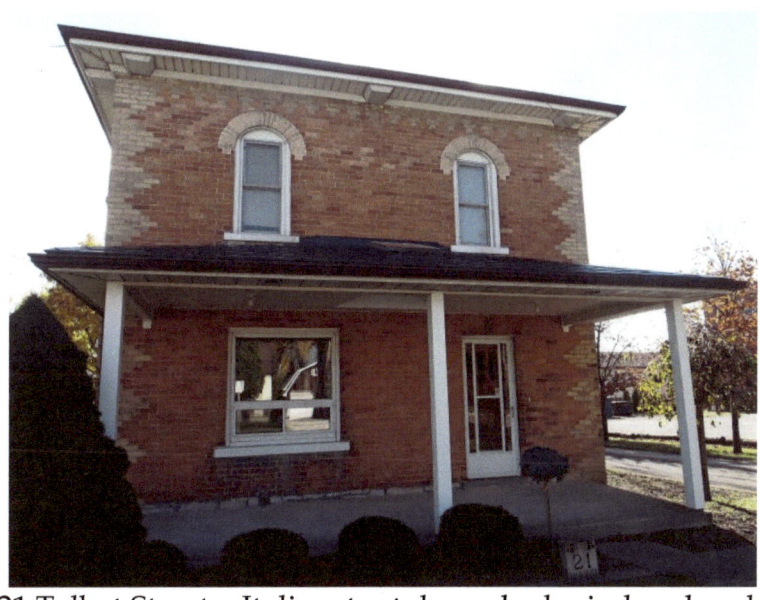

21 Talbot Street – Italianate style, arched window hoods

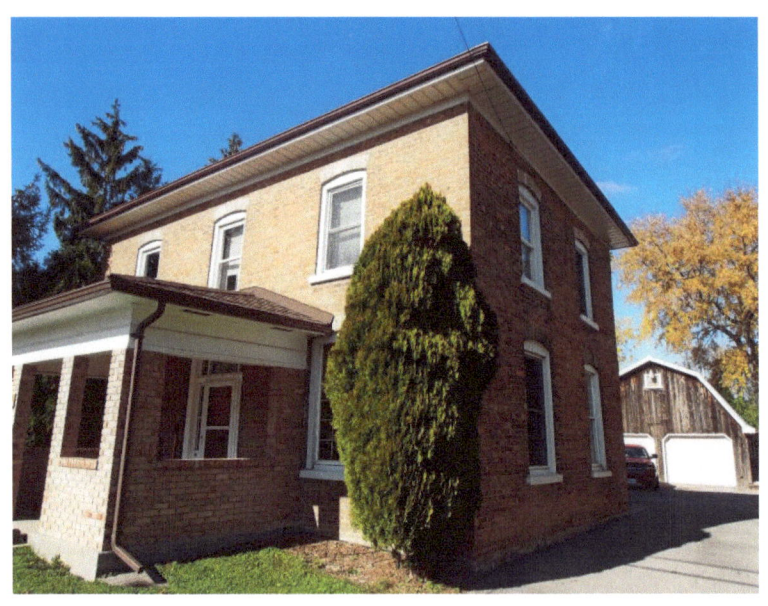

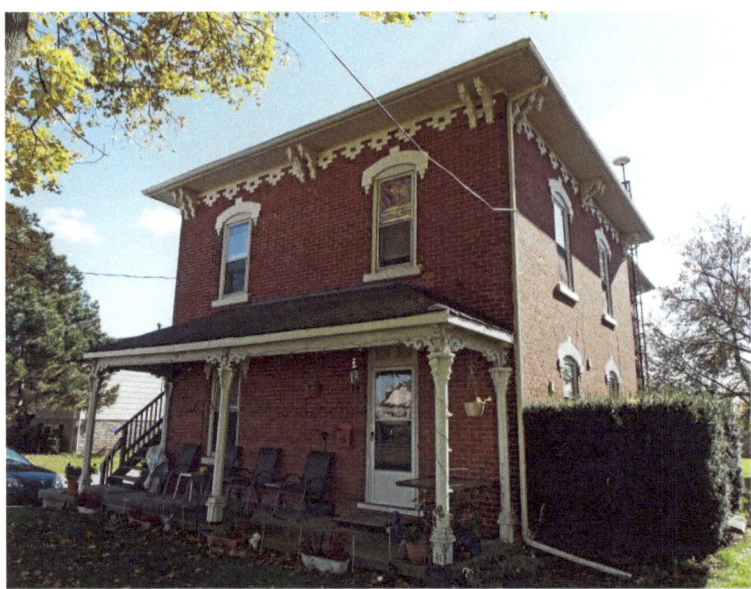

53 Talbot Street – Italianate style, paired cornice brackets, dichromatic patterning below cornice, arched window hoods

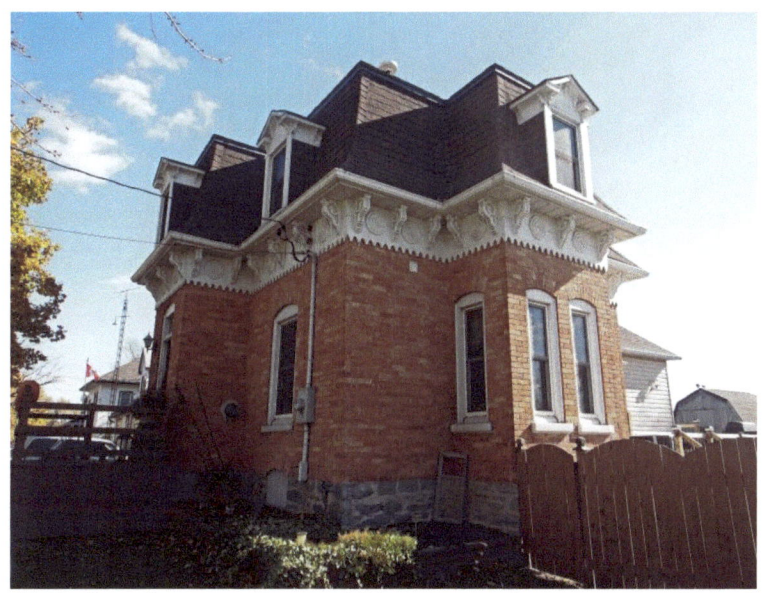

45 Talbot Street – Second Empire style – mansard roof, dormers in roof, single cornice brackets, cornice return on small gables on window dormers

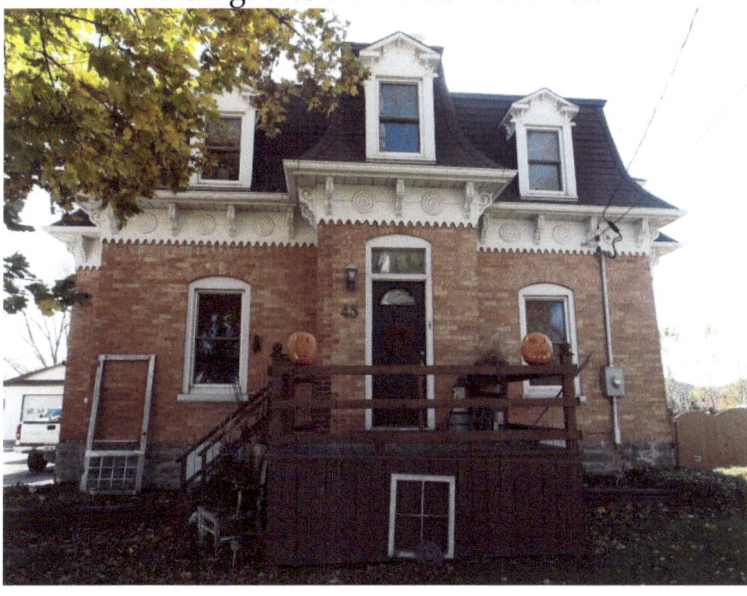

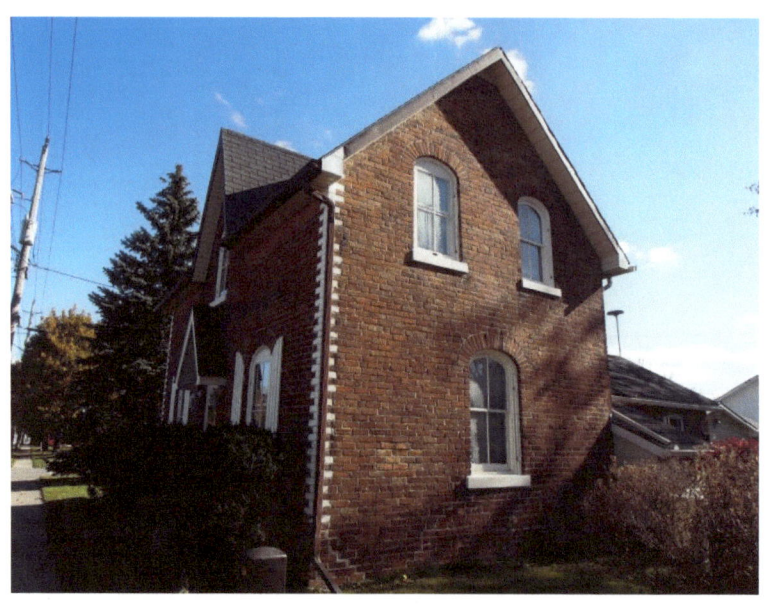

#31 Talbot Street – Gothic Revival – 1½ storeys, arched voussoirs

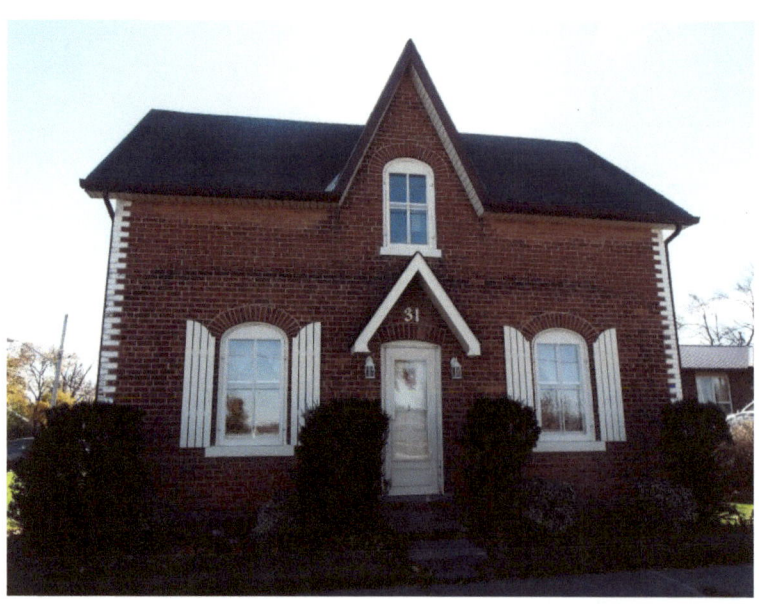

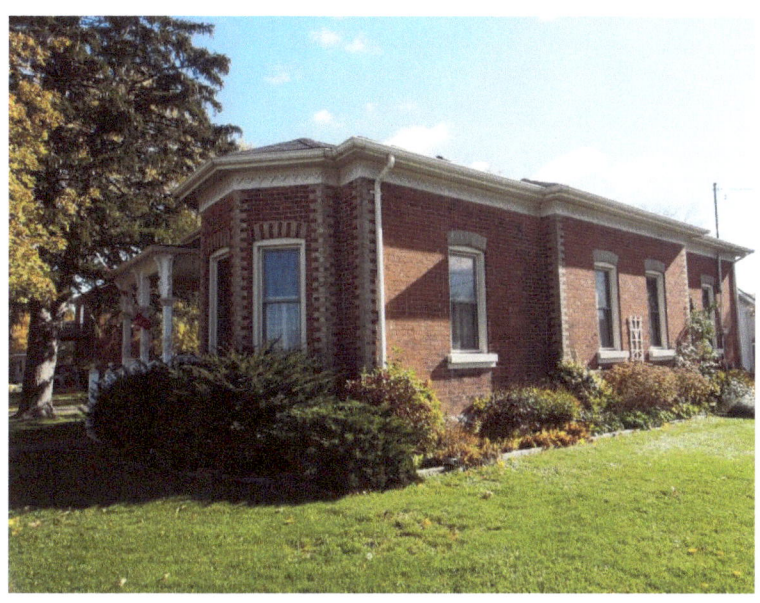

25 Talbot Street – dichromatic brickwork, corner quoins – Italianate style – unusual one floor only

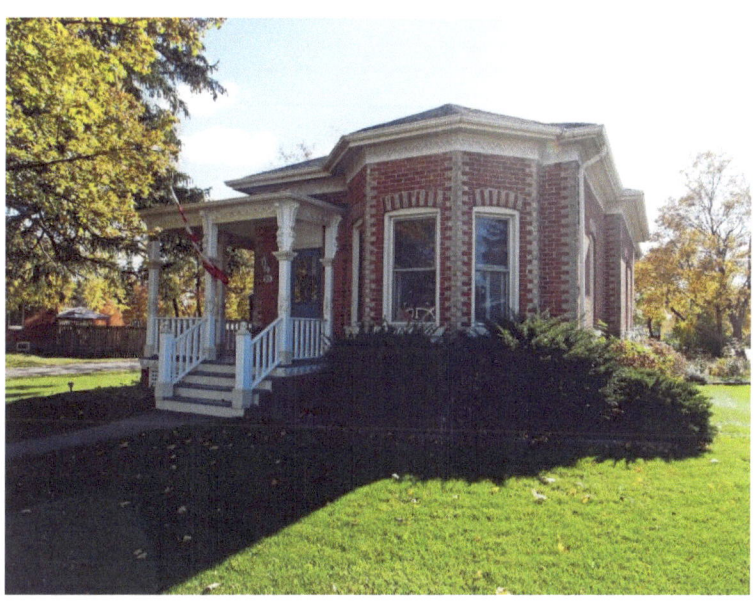

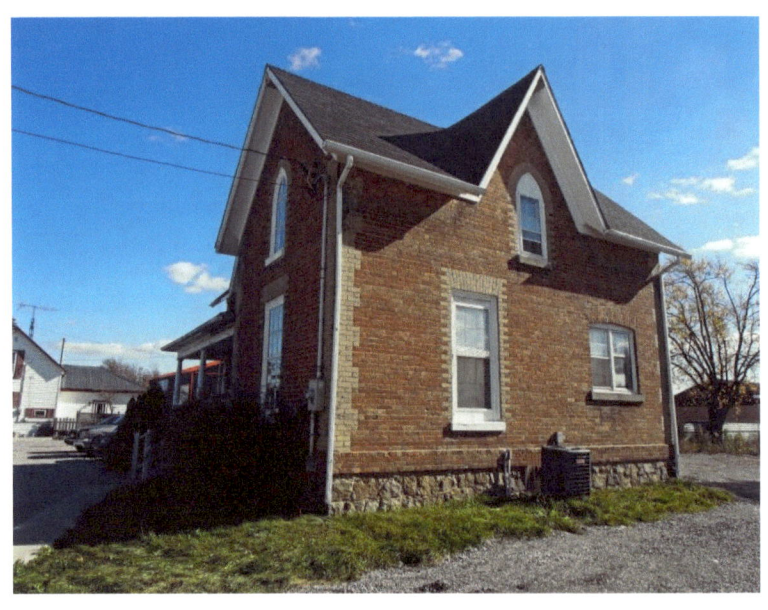

Gothic Revival style – dichromatic brickwork

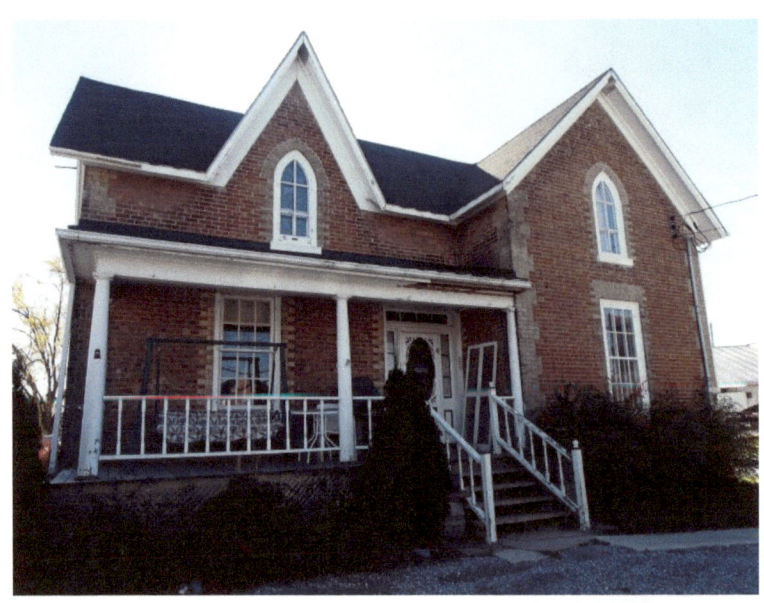

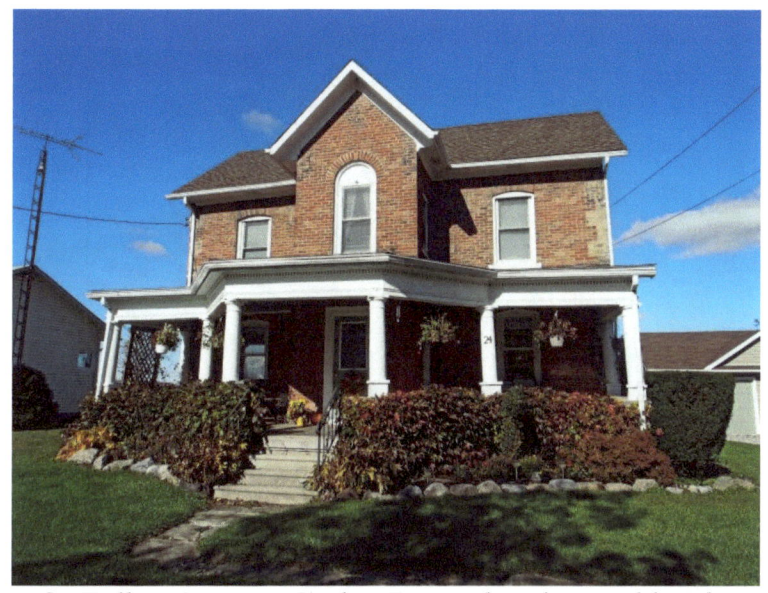

24 Talbot Street – Gothic Revival style – red brick, corner quoins

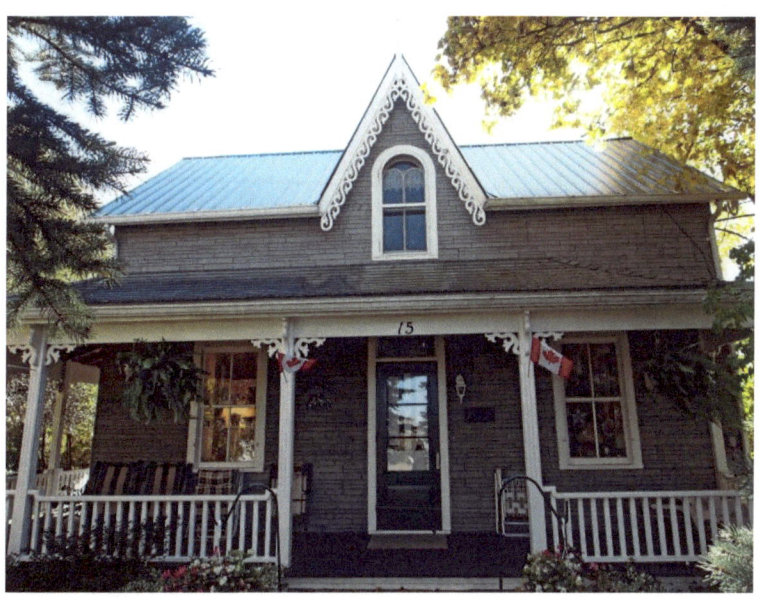

15 Talbot Street – Gothic Revival, Vergeboard trim and finial on gable

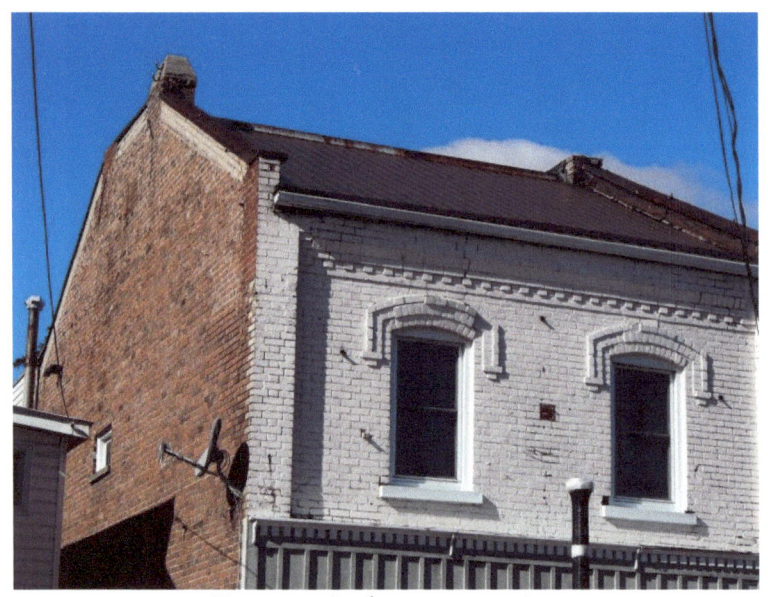

Fancy window voussoirs

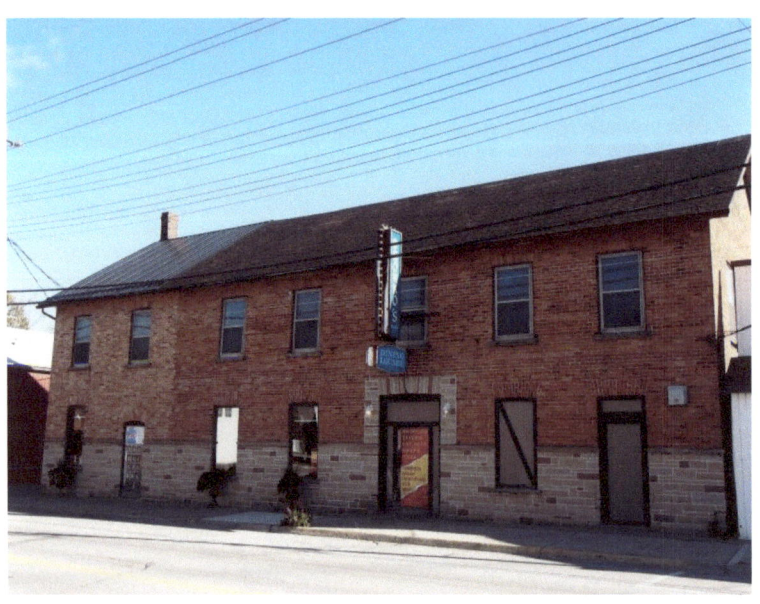

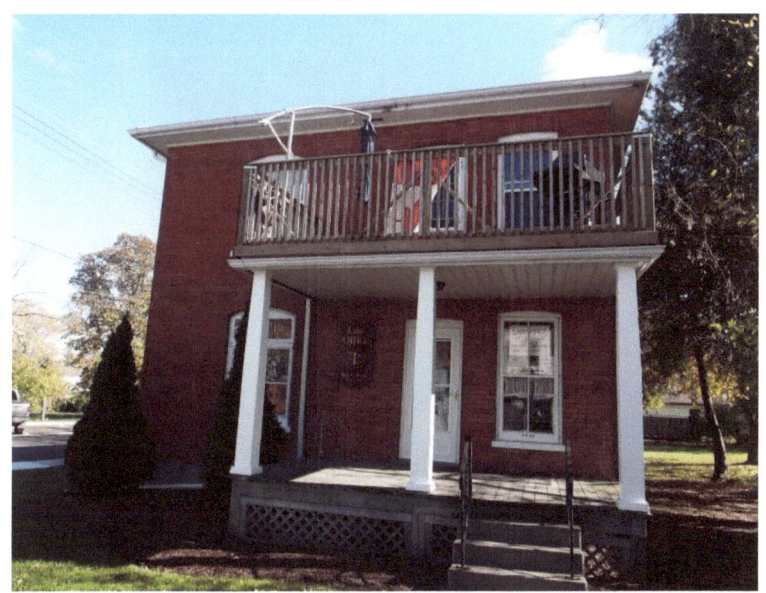

Italianate style

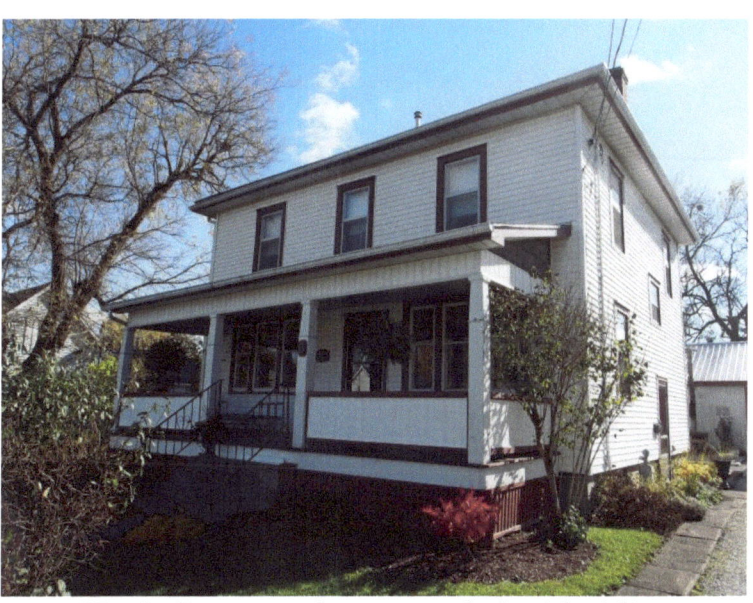

#8 – Italianate style – upgraded with siding

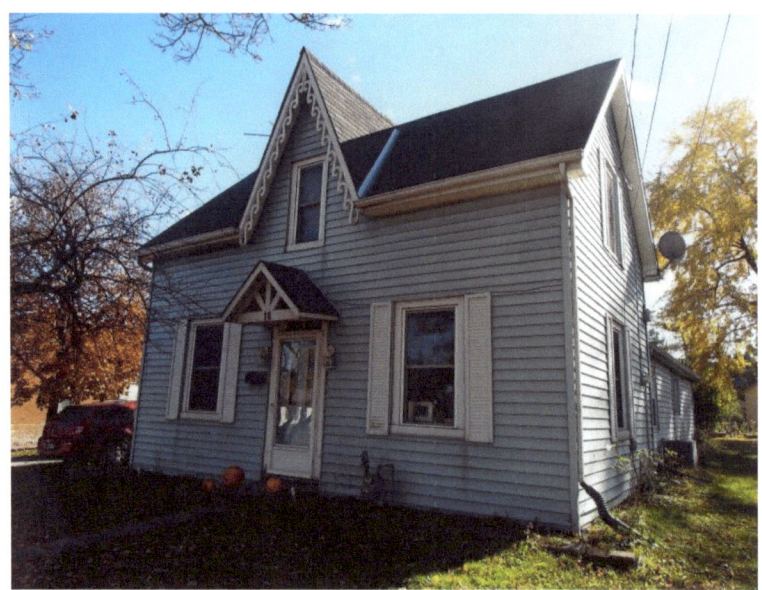

#10 - Gothic Revival with Vergeboard trim on the attic gable

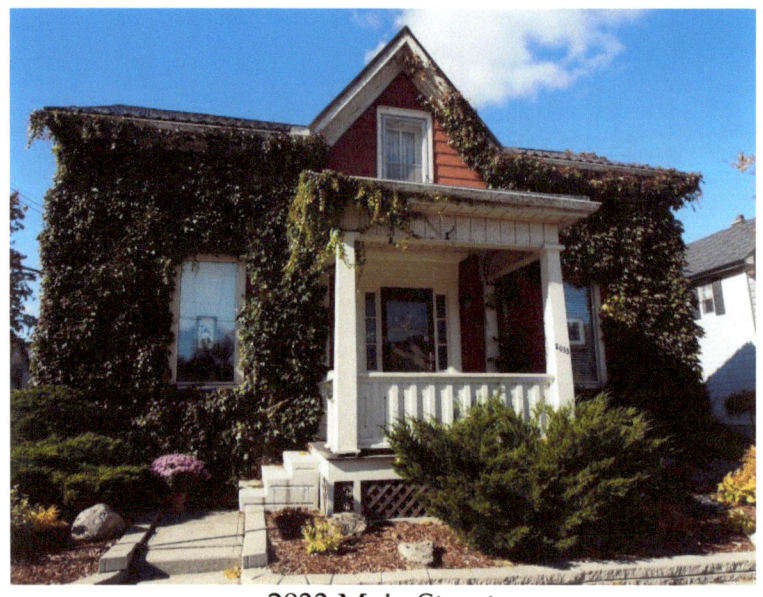

2033 Main Street

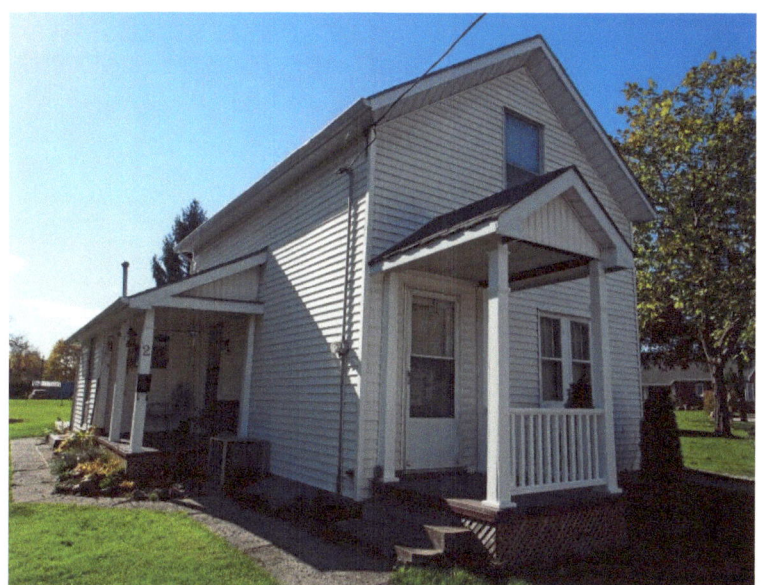

2 Peel Street

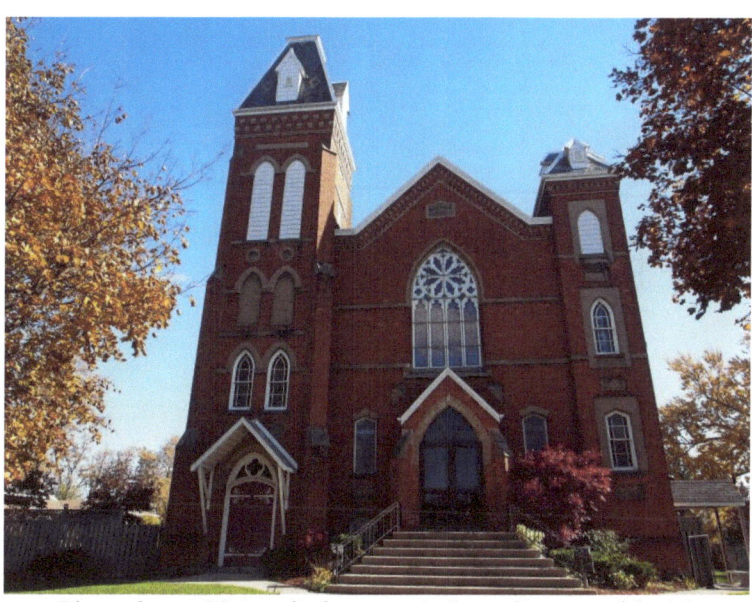

Knox Church – 1896 – dichromatic banding and brickwork,
dichromatic tile work in tower

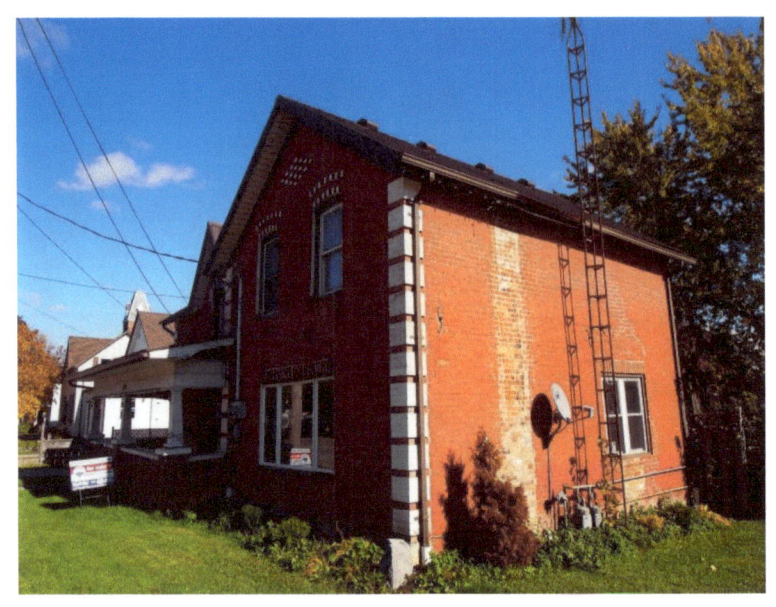

2046 Main Street

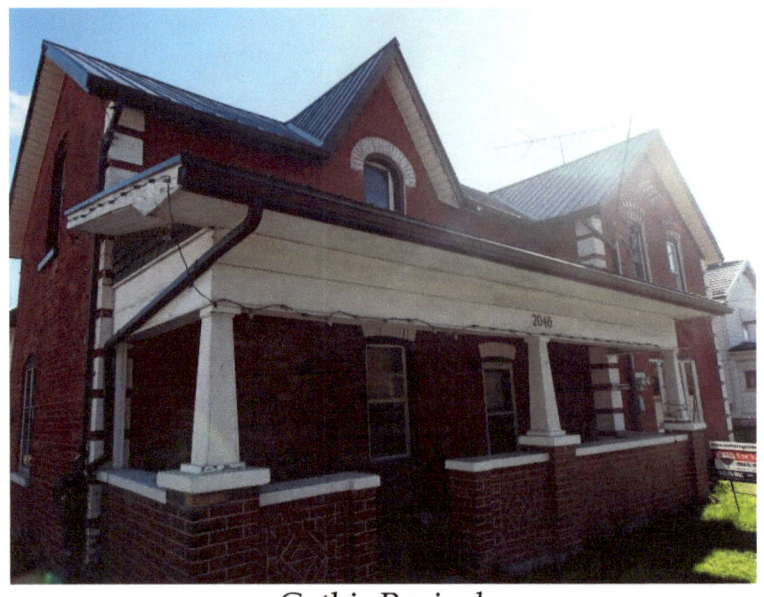

Gothic Revival

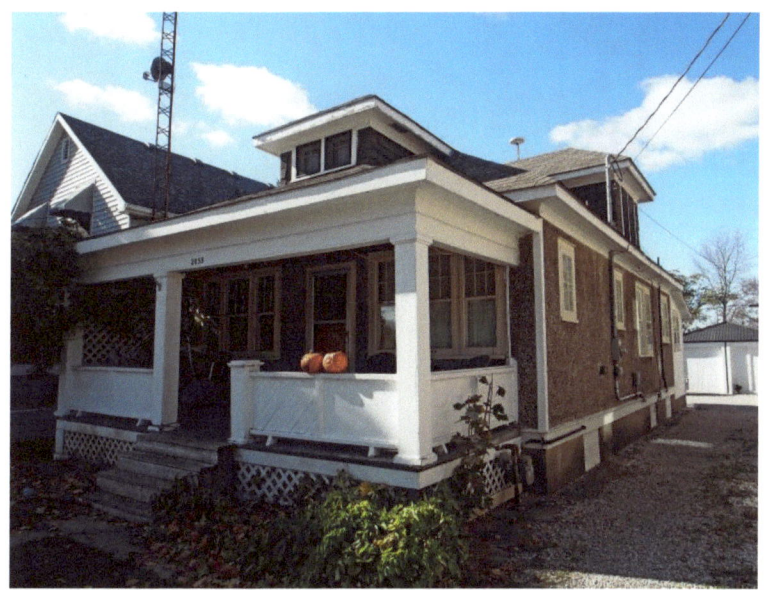

2055 Main Street – Italianate – dormer in roof – stucco exterior

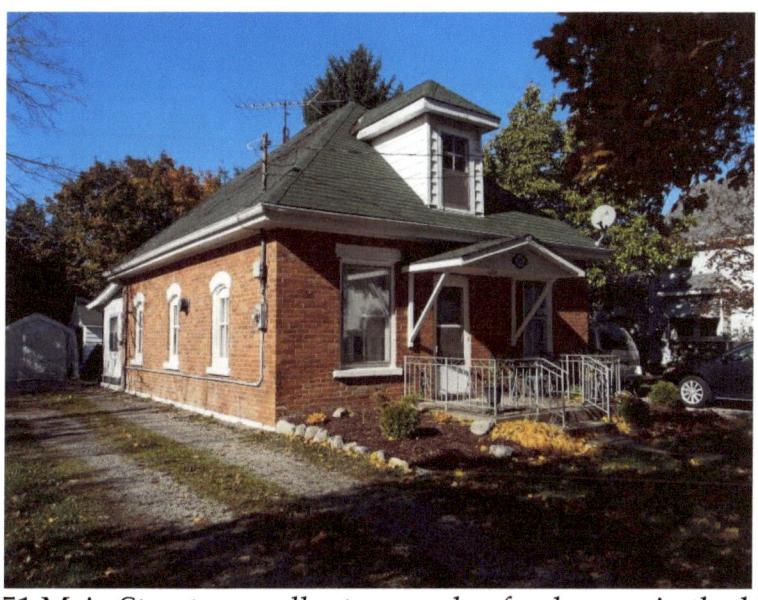

2051 Main Street – excellent example of a dormer in the hip roof – Italianate style

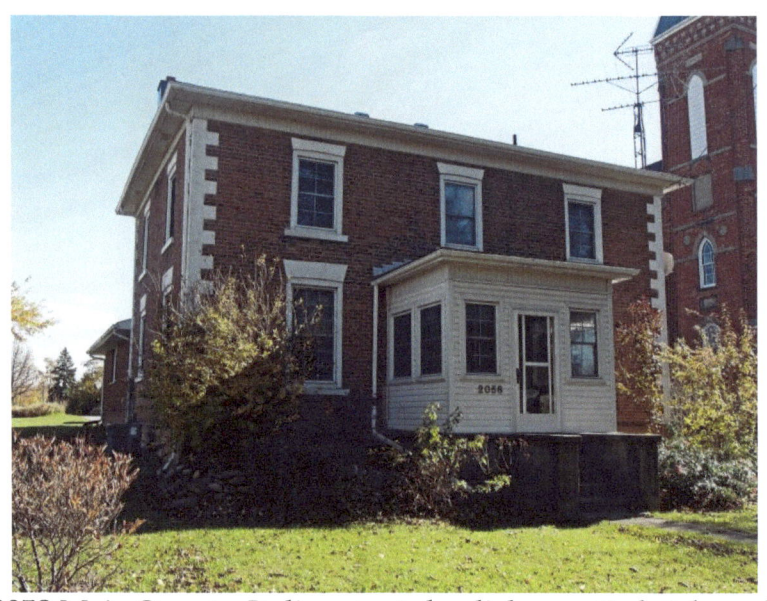

2058 Main Street – Italianate style, dichromatic brickwork

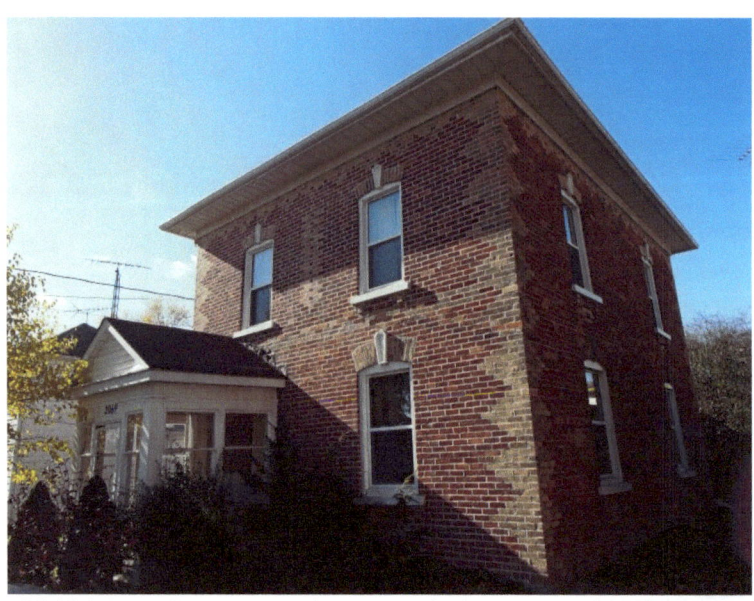

2069 Main Street – Italianate, dichromatic brickwork,
voussoirs with keystones

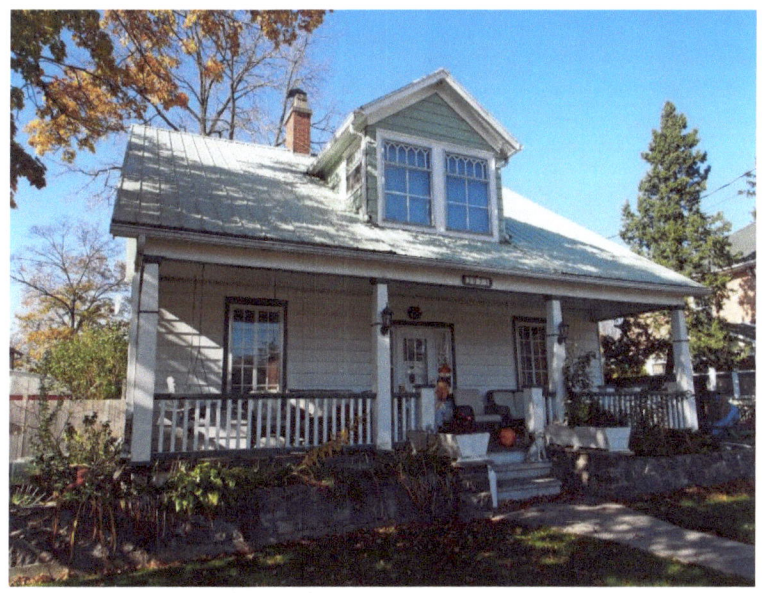

2073 Main Street – dormer in attic – Gothic cottage

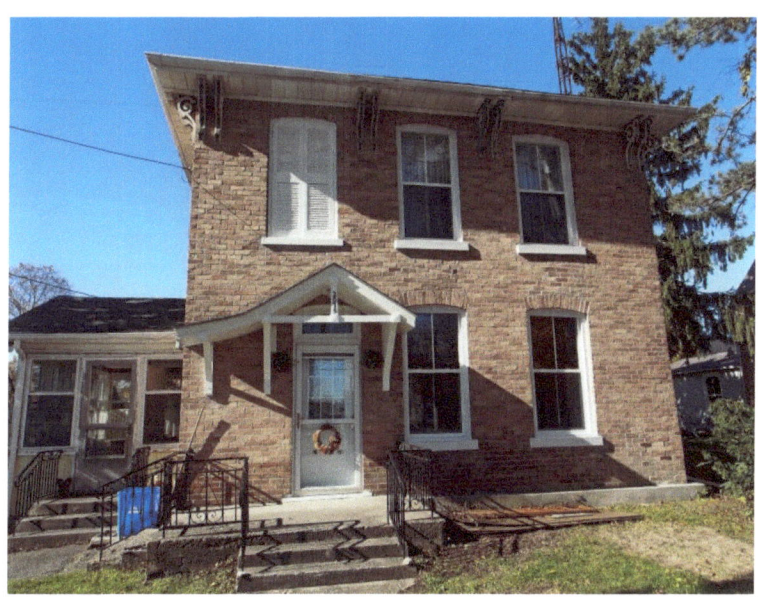

2075 Main Street – Italianate style with paired cornice brackets

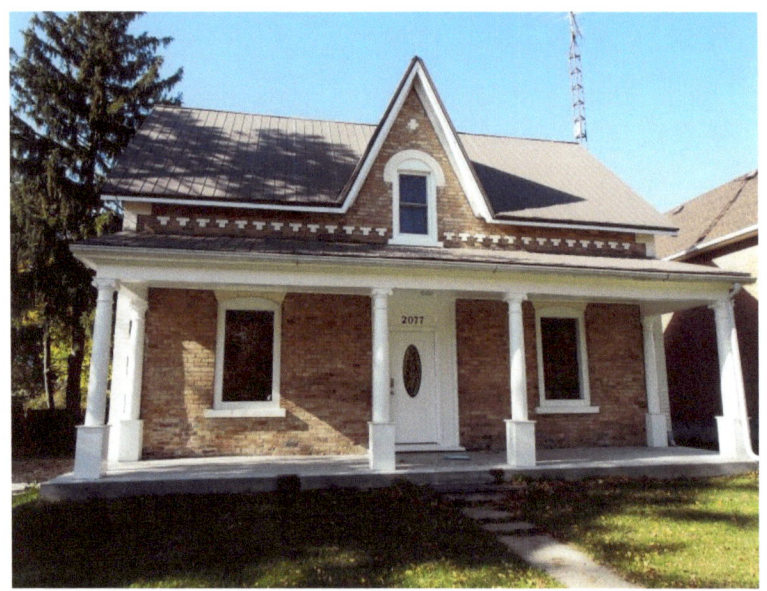

2077 Main Street – arched window hood in attic gable – Gothic cottage, light red brick, decorative brickwork below cornice

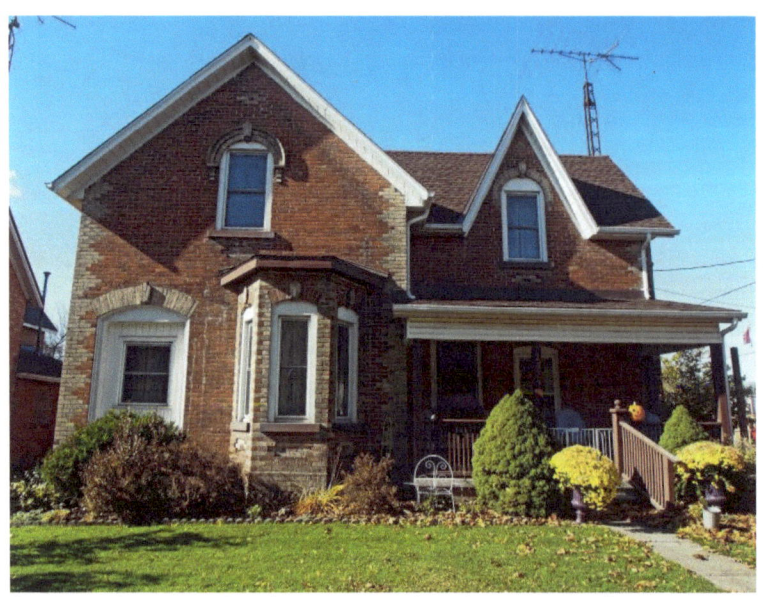

2079 Main Street - Gothic Revival – decorative keystones and voussoirs, bay window, dichromatic brickwork

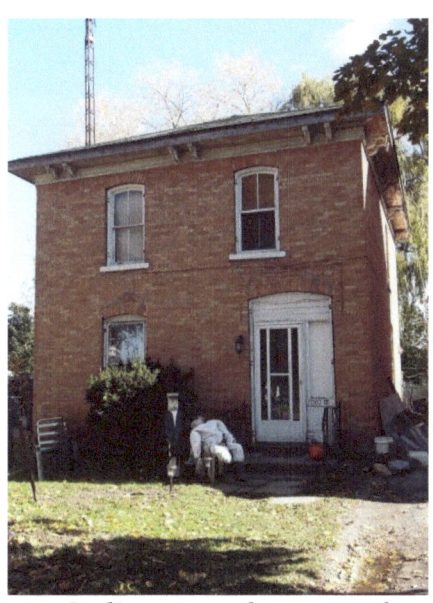

2080 Main Street – Italianate style – paired cornice brackets, orange/red brick

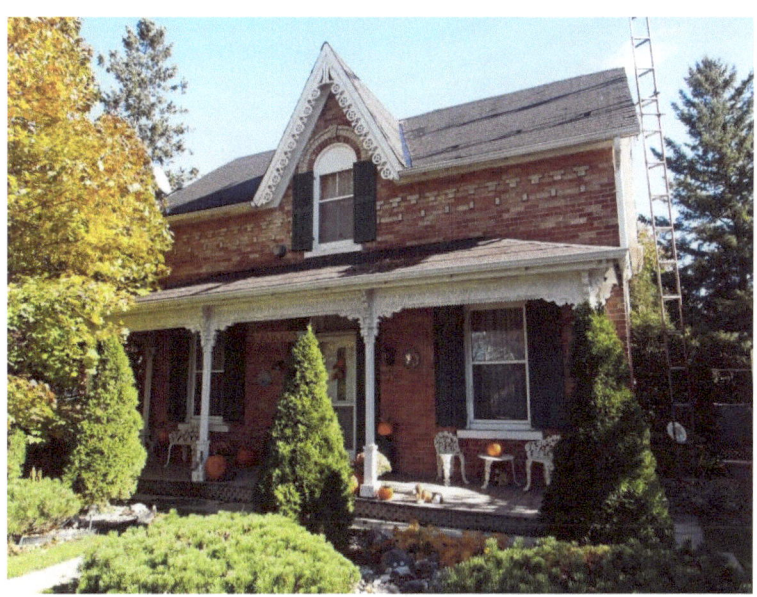

Gothic Revival – Vergeboard trim on gable, arched voussoirs and keystones, orange/red brick, decorative brickwork below cornice – "Meadwood"

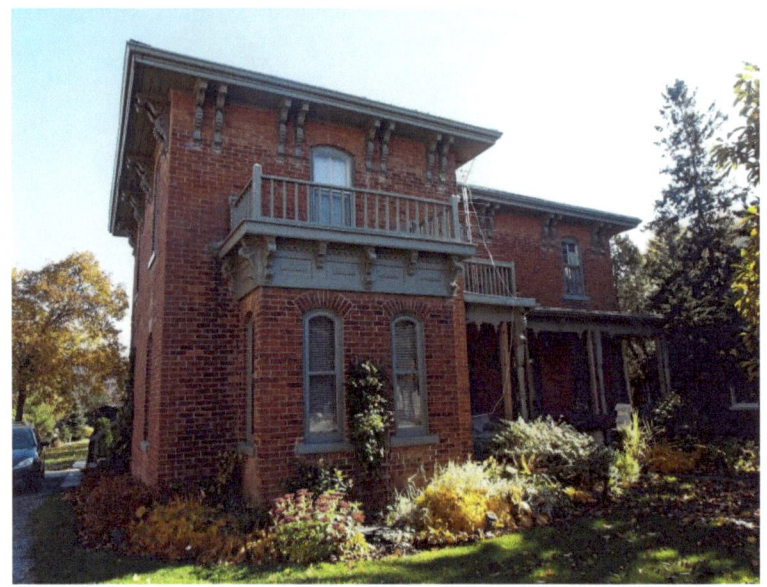

2086 Main Street – Italianate – paired cornice brackets, arched voussoirs, red brick

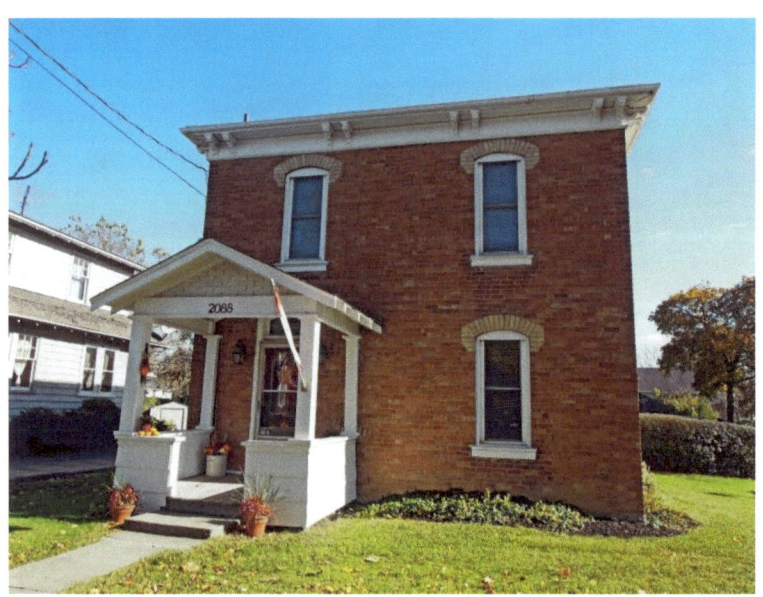

2088 Main Street – two storey, Italianate, arched window hoods, paired cornice brackets

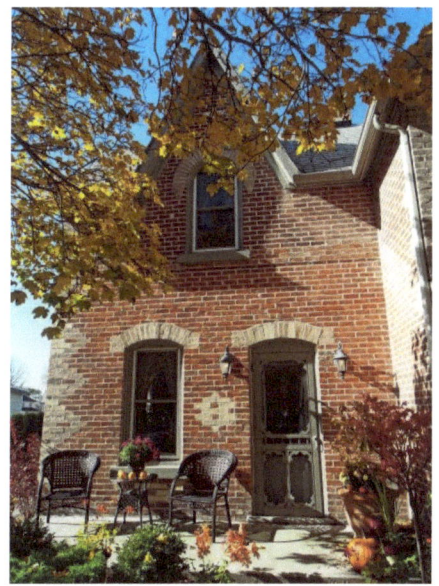

Gothic Revival – dichromatic brickwork

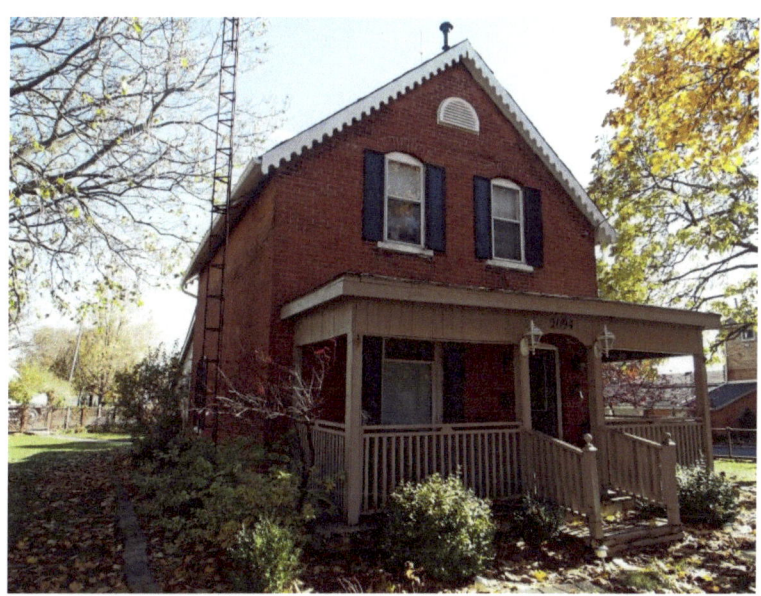

2094 Main Street – Vergeboard trim on gable

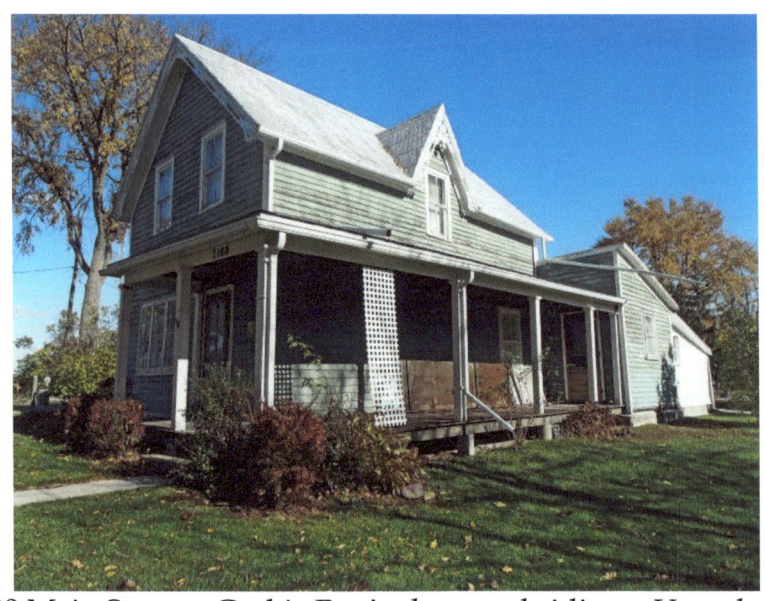

2100 Main Street – Gothic Revival – wood siding – Vergeboard trim on gables

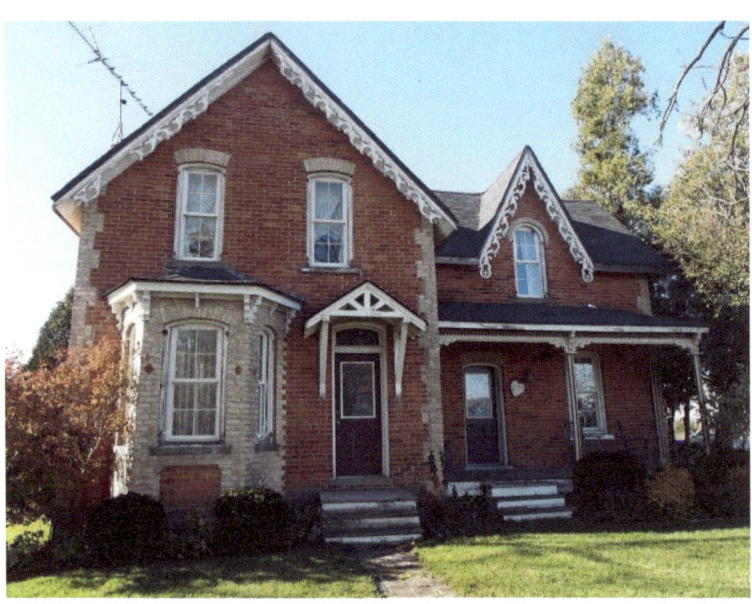

2145 Main Street - Gothic Revival – Vergeboard trim, bay window with cornice brackets

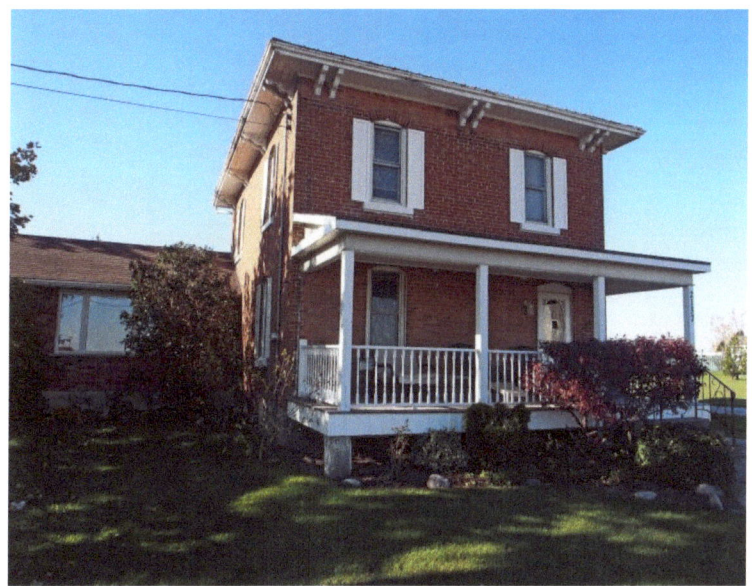

2137 Main Street – Italianate

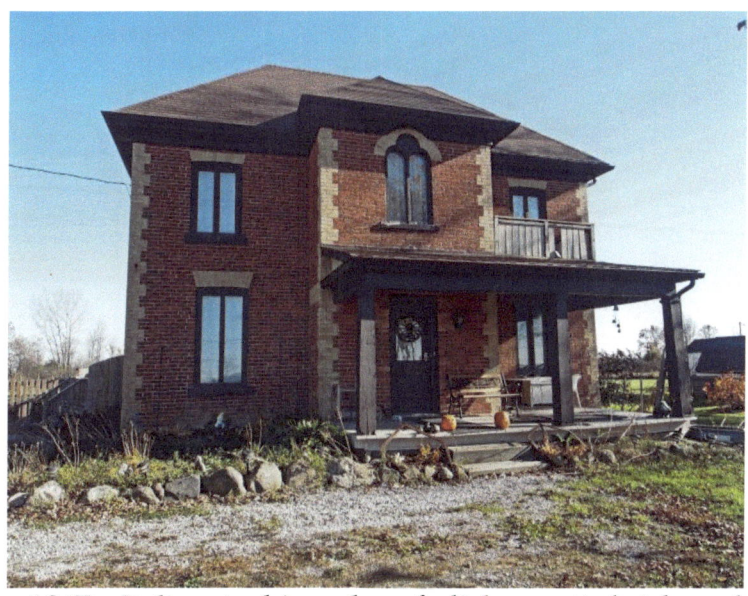

c. 1847 – Italianate, hipped roof, dichromatic brickwork

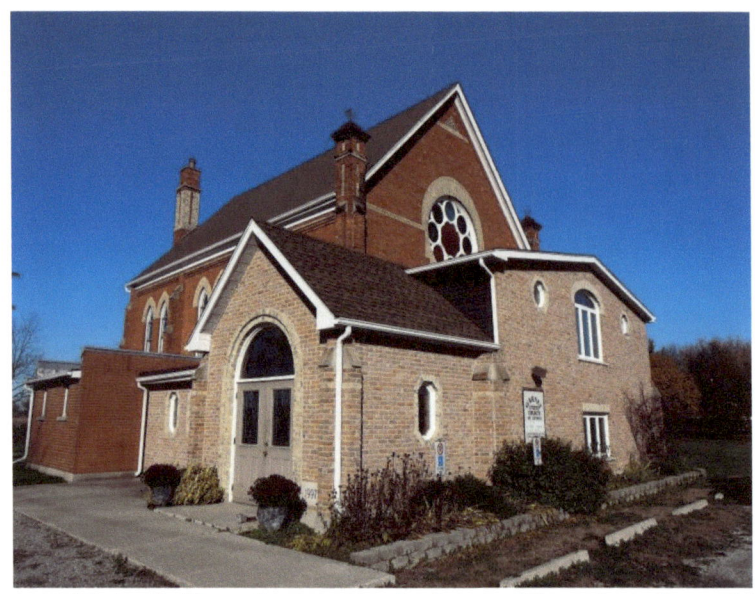

Garnet United Church – rose window with red, yellow, blue,
green, navy, and magenta circles – back portion c. 1889
(Methodist Church), front addition 1997

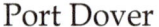

Port Dover

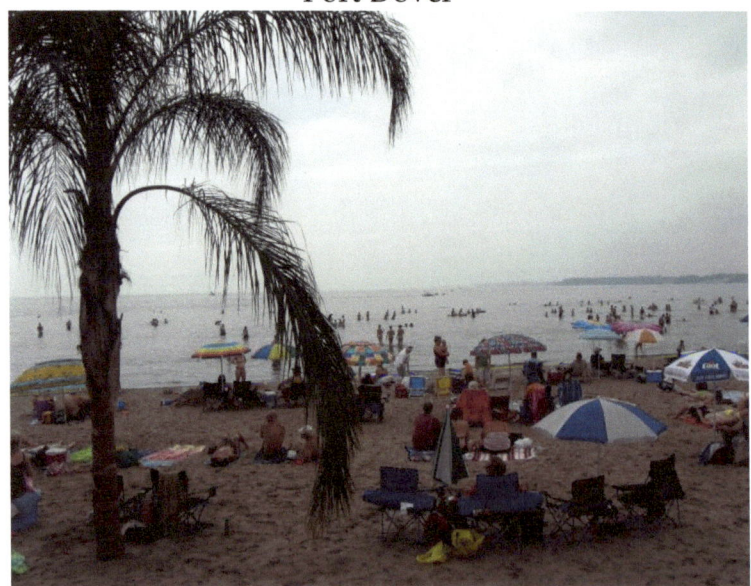

Lake Erie Beach

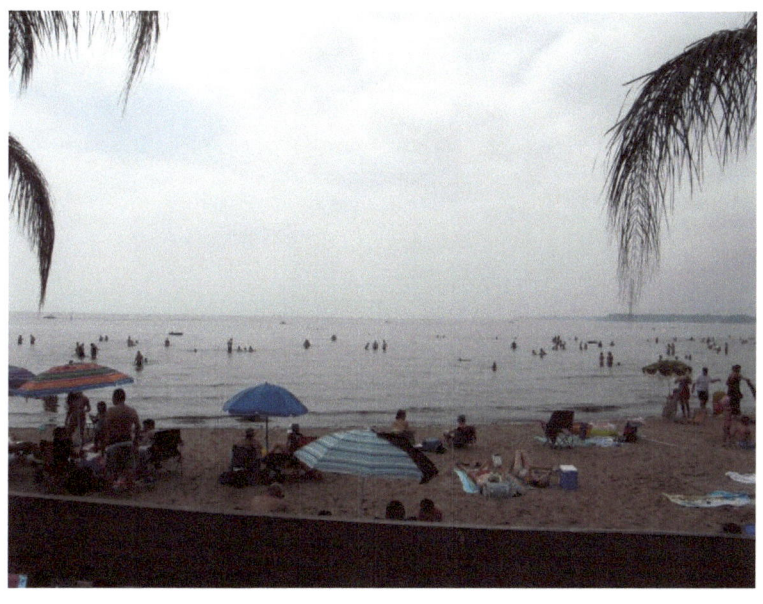

A hot summer day calls for time on the beach at Port Dover.

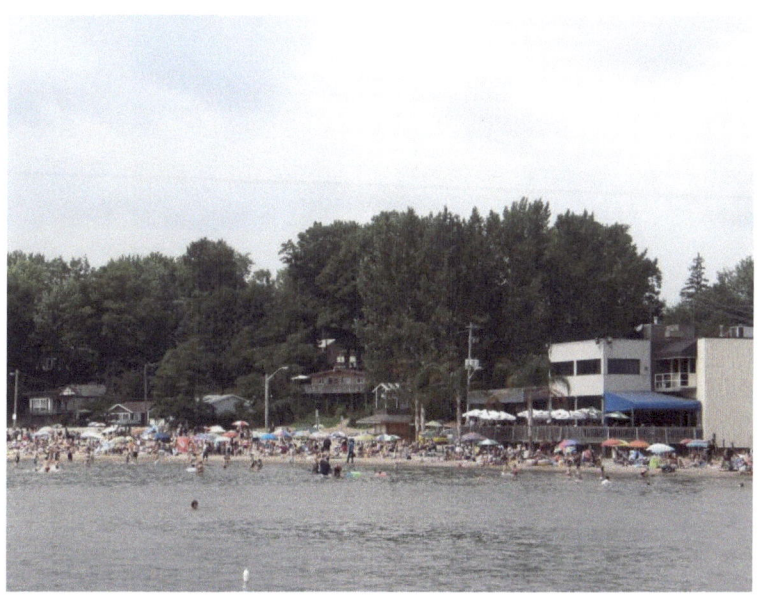

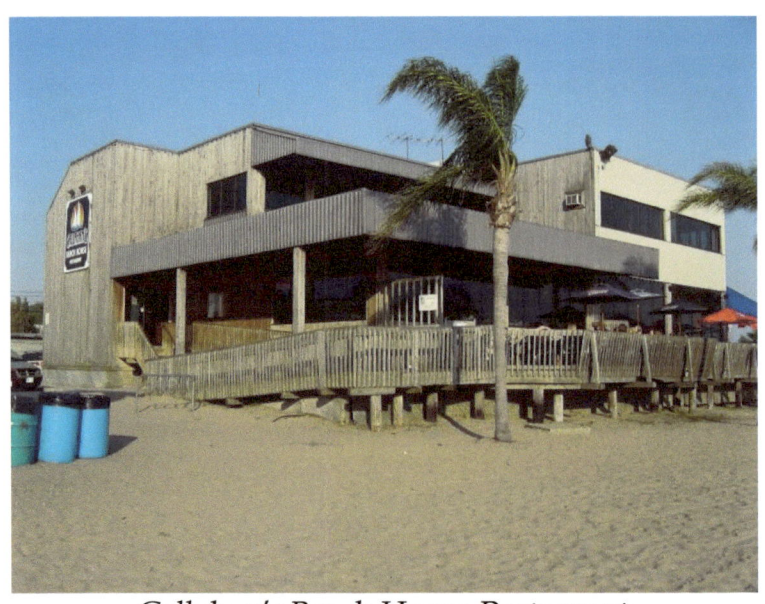

Callahan's Beach House Restaurant
– a great place for Lake Erie perch

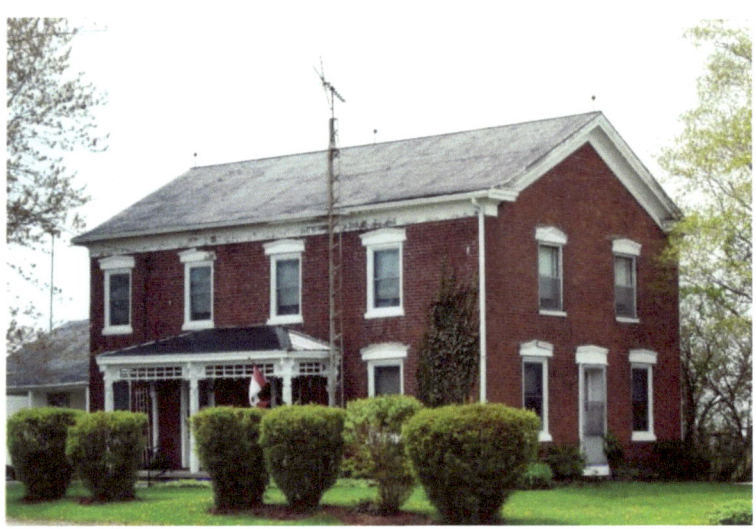

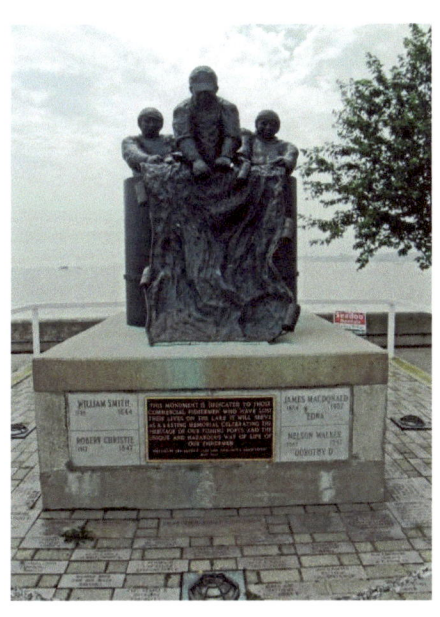

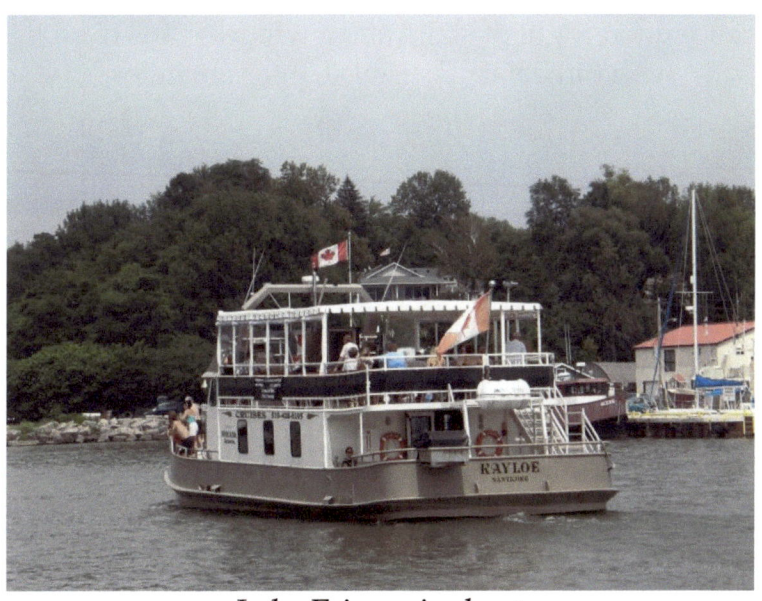

Lake Erie cruise boat

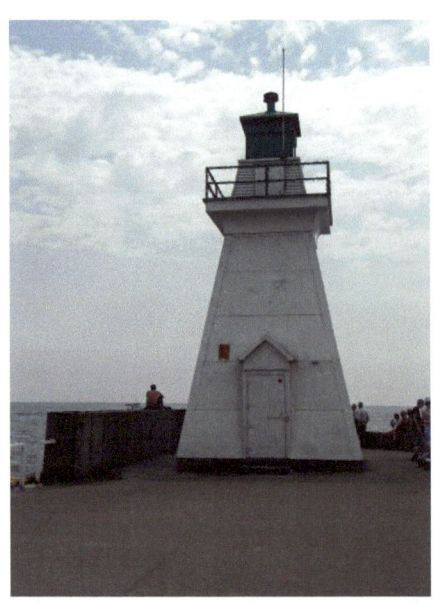

One of the oldest examples of pre-Confederation small harbour lighthouses surviving in Ontario – a simple square wooden tower, tapered slightly at the top, with a single entrance door, flight of stairs and a window. It's fixed light with three burners is visible for ten miles.

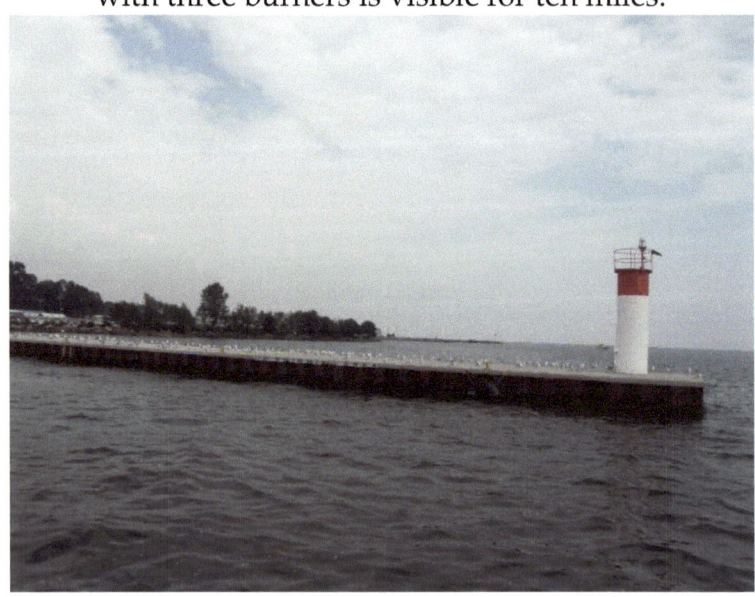

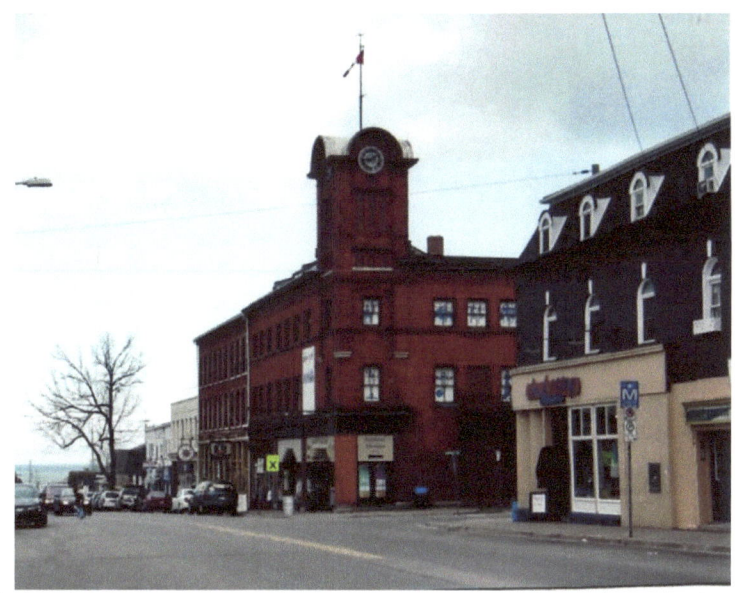

Dark building to right of picture – mansard roof with dormers

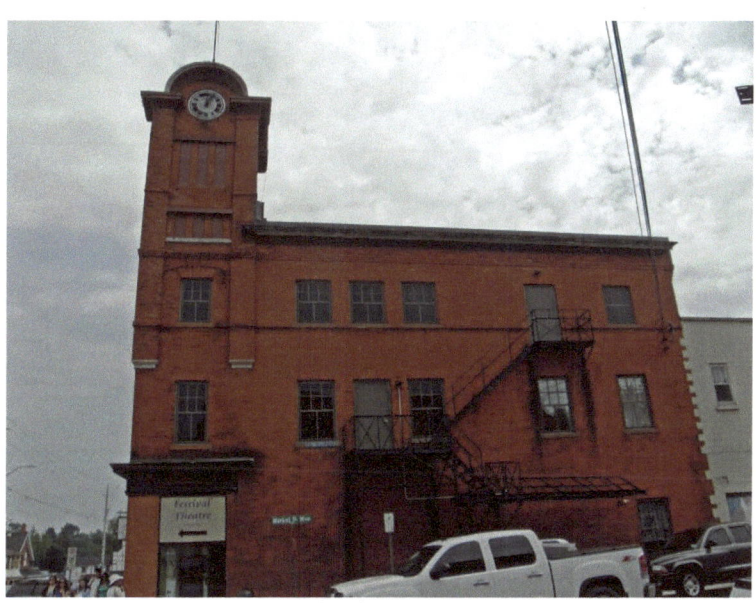

Clock tower

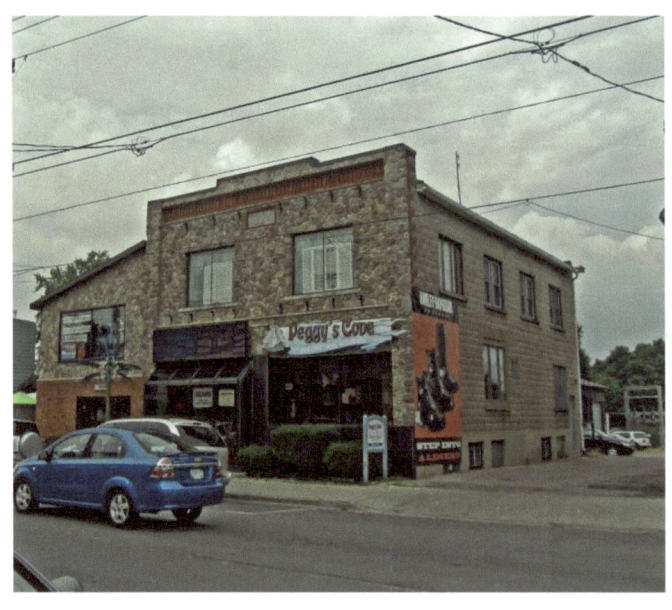

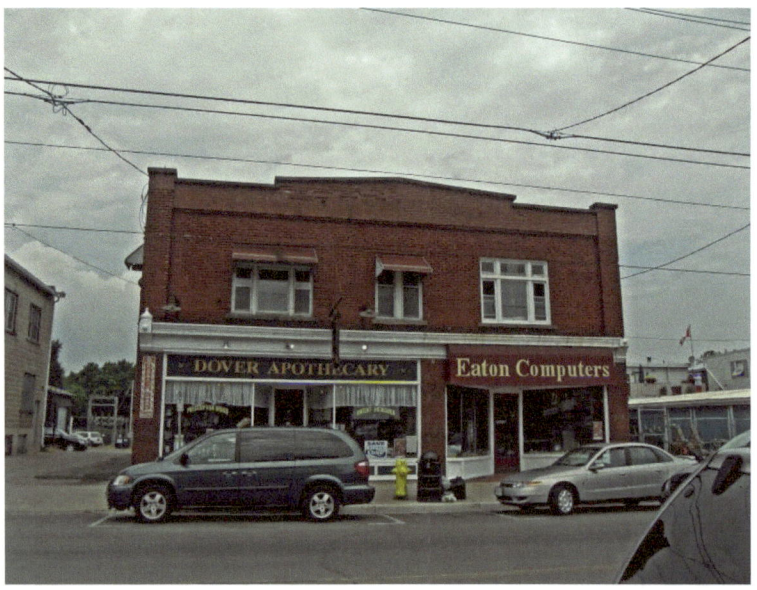

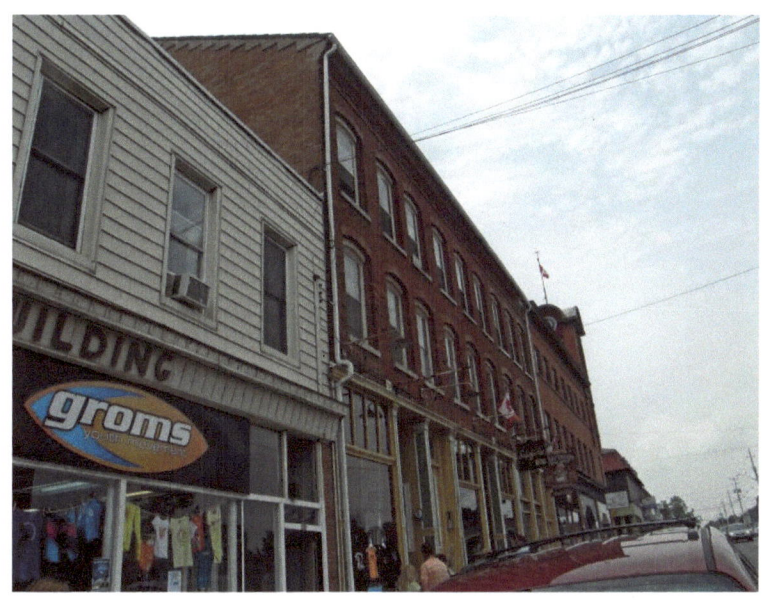

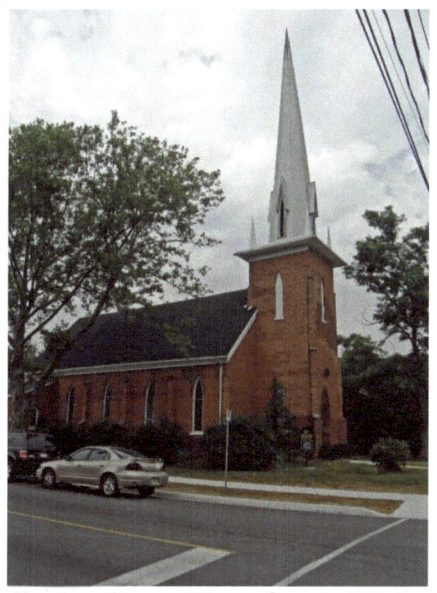

St. Paul's Anglican Church established 1852

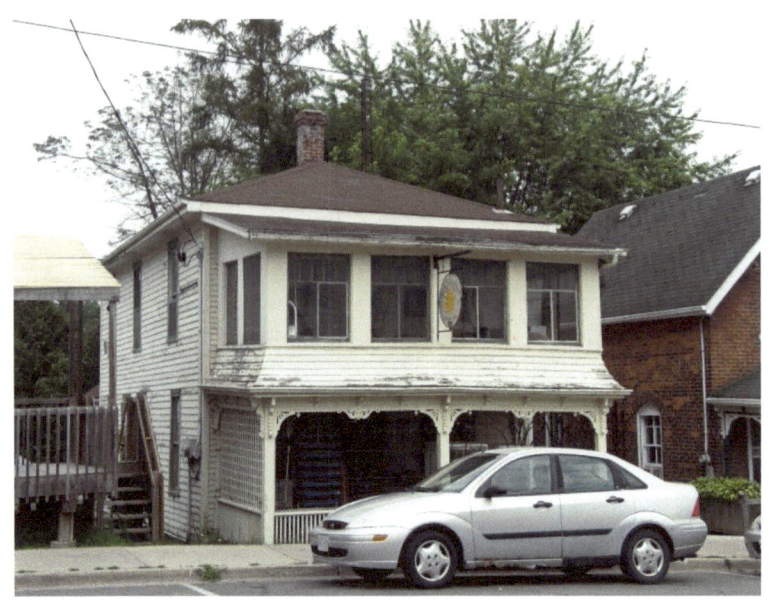

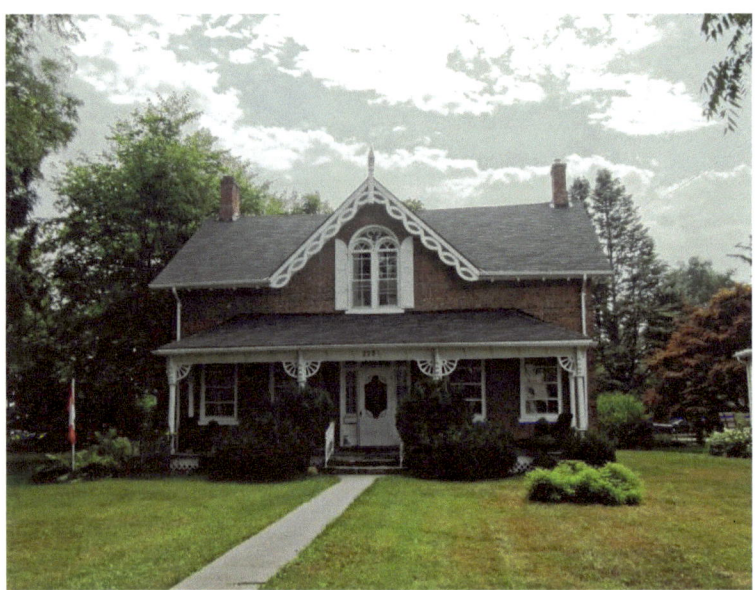

Gothic Revival – Vergeboard trim and finial on gable

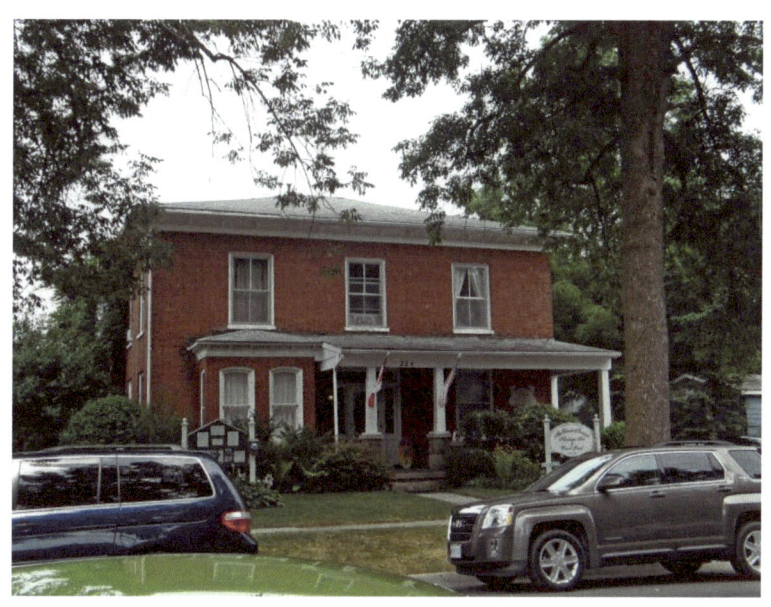

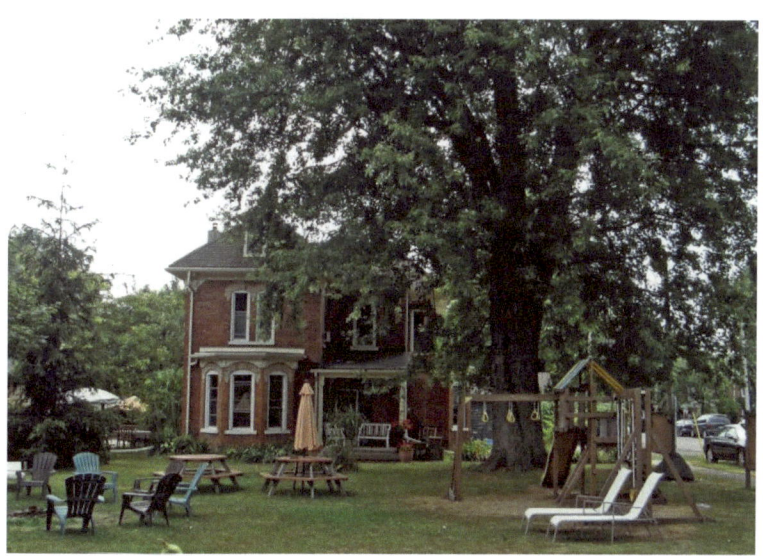

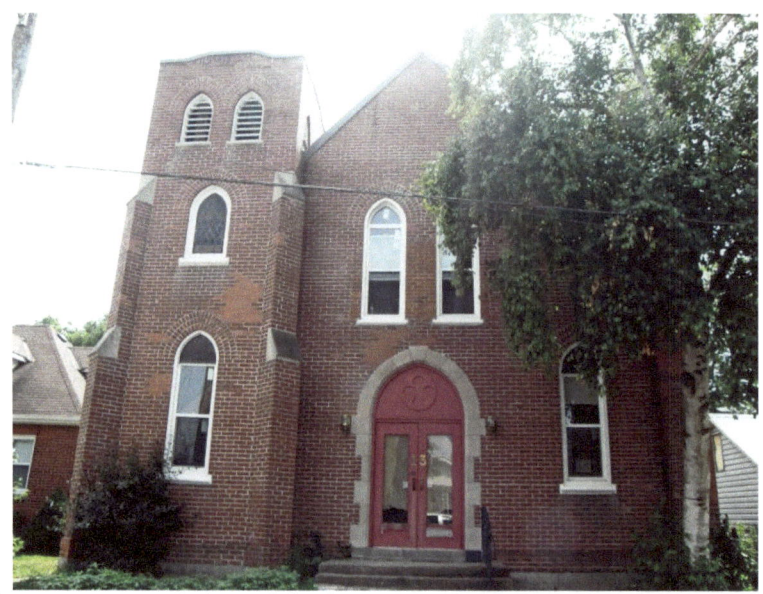

The sanctuary and altar of the former St. Cecilia's Catholic Church were built in 1898. A large two storey addition in the front of the building and a smaller one behind the altar were added in 1932. The building ceased as a church in the early 1970s. In 2010, four apartments were created.

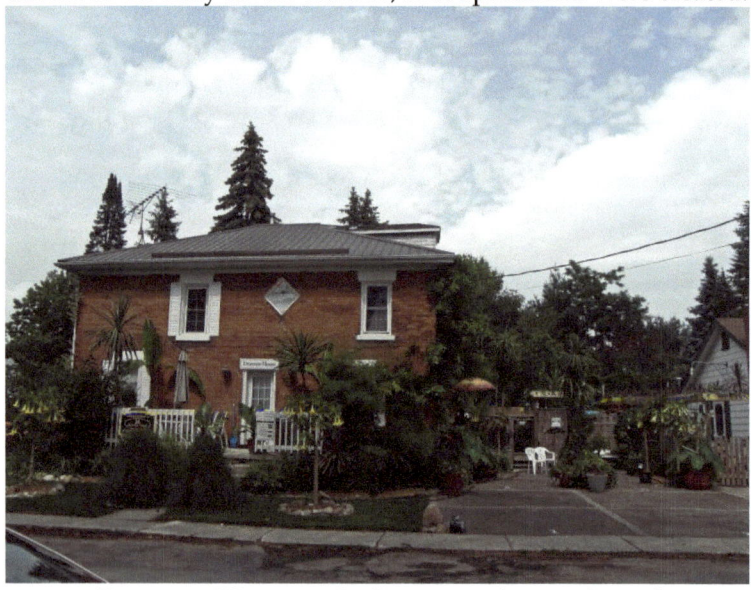

Drayton House – Italianate – hipped roof

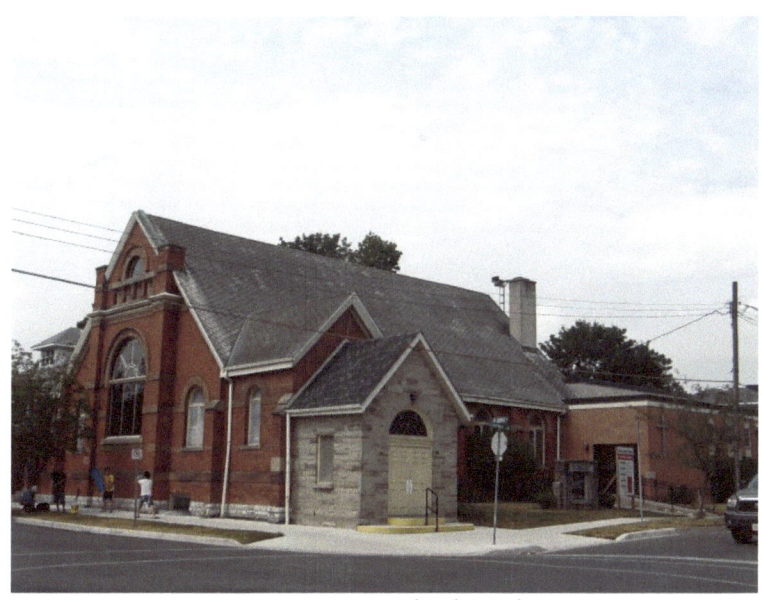

Grace United Church

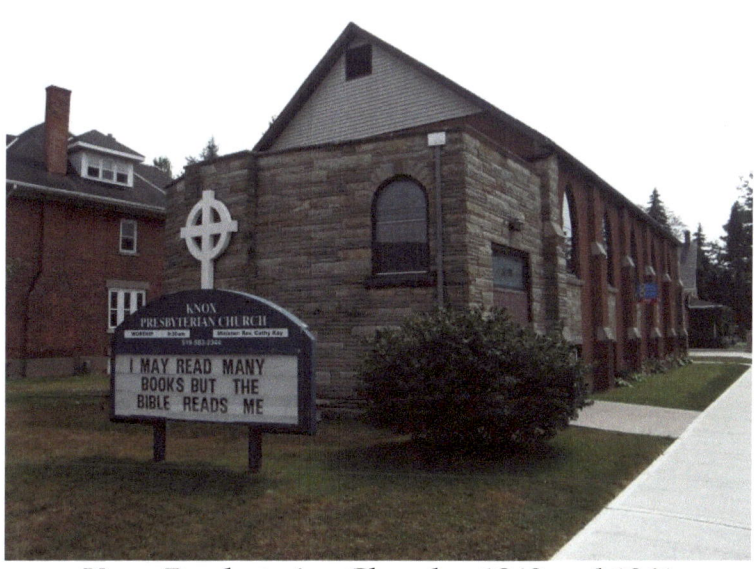

Knox Presbyterian Church – 1849 and 1961

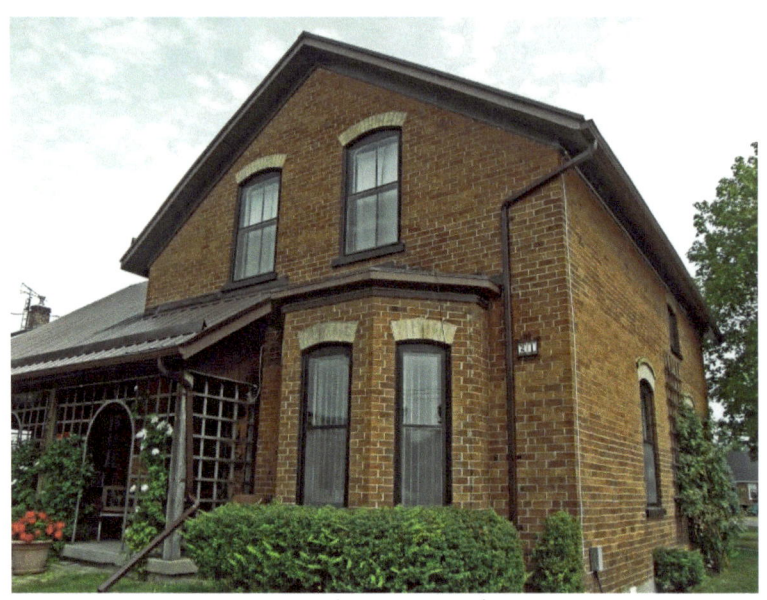

Gothic Revival

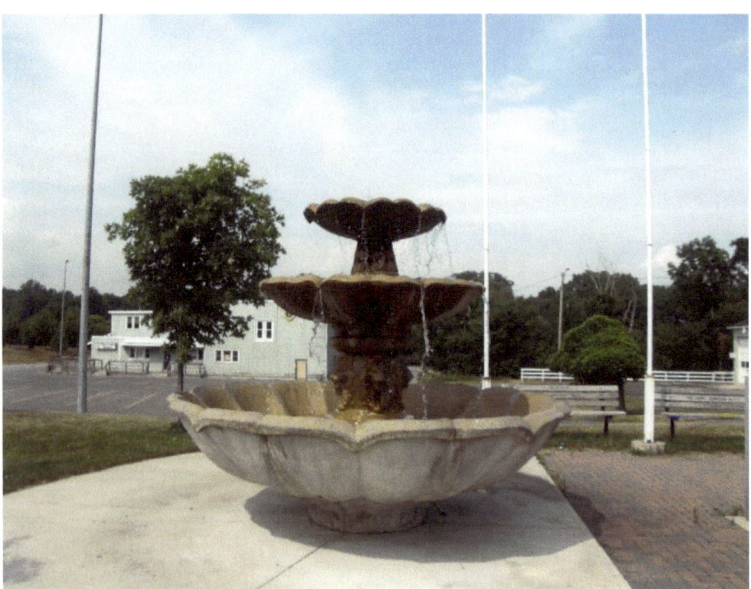

Fountain at Silver Lake Park

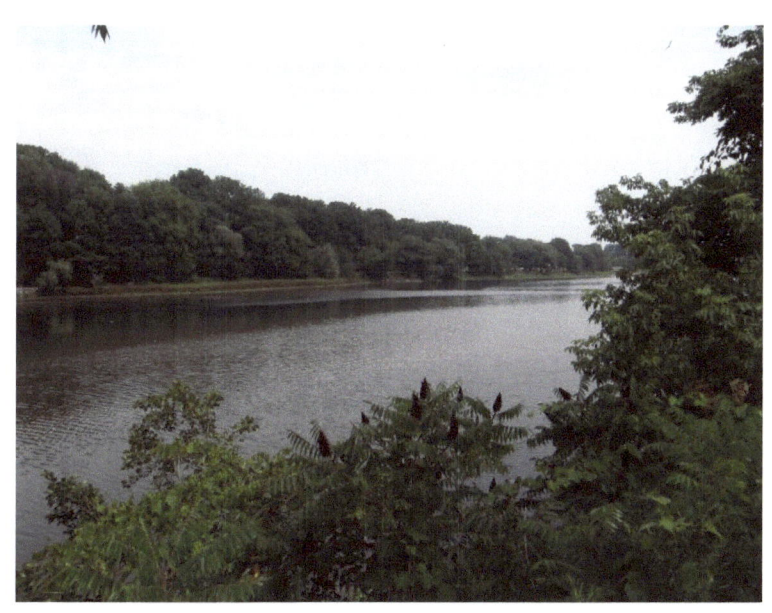

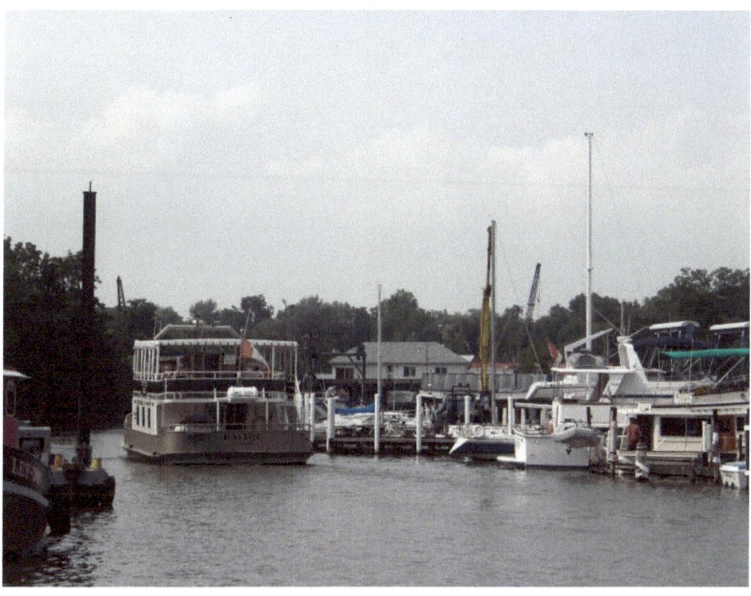

Architectural Terms

Brackets: a decorative or weight-bearing structural element which forms a right angle with one side against a wall and the other under a projecting surface such as an eave or roof. Example: 2075 Main Street, Jarvis	
Cobblestone architecture: Refers to the use of cobblestones embedded in mortar as a method for erecting walls on houses and commercial buildings. Example: Wesley United Church, Jarvis	
Cornice: originally the wooden overhang of the roof. With the use of stone, brick, iron and steel, the cornice is any projecting shelf at the top of a ceiling or roof. They can be very decorative. Example: 45 Talbot Street, Jarvis	
Cornice Return: decorative element on the end of a gable. Example: 45 Talbot Street, Jarvis	
Dentil Moulding: an even series of rectangles used as ornamental decoration in cornices. Example: Knox Church, Jarvis	
Dichromatic brickwork: the use of two colours of brick, tile or slate to decorate a façade. Example: 53 Talbot Street, Jarvis	

Dormer: (French for "sleep") a gable end window that pierces through the plane of a sloping roof surface to create usable space in the top floor or attic of a building by adding headroom. Example: 2150 Main Street, Jarvis	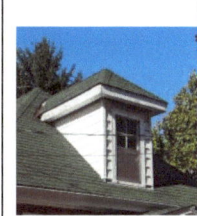
Gable: the triangular portion of a wall between the edges of a sloping roof. Example: 2094 Main Street, Jarvis	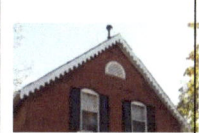
Hipped Roof: a roof where all sides slope downwards to the walls with no gables.	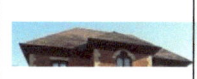
Keystones and Voussoirs: a voussoir is a wedge-shaped element used in building an arch. A keystone is the central stone that locks all the stones into position, allowing the arch to bear weight. A keystone is often enlarged and embellished. Example: 2079 Main Street, Jarvis	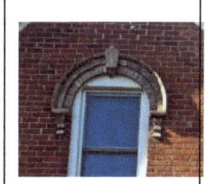
Lancet Window: a tall, narrow window with a pointed arch at its top. Example: Knox Church, Jarvis	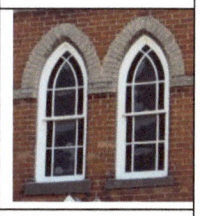
Mansard Roof: This style was popularized by Francois Mansart (1598-1666), an accomplished architect of the French Baroque period and especially fashionable during the Second French Empire (1852-1870). This roof is almost flat on the top section, with two slopes on each of its sides with the lower slope at a steeper angle than the upper and having dormer windows. Example: 45 Talbot Street, Jarvis	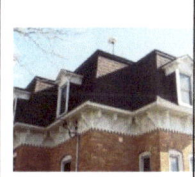

Pediment: a triangular section above the horizontal structure (entablature), typically supported by columns. The inside of the triangle is called the tympanum. Example: 60 Talbot Street East, Jarvis	
Quoin: masonry blocks at the corner of a wall, often a decorative feature, usually larger or of a different colour than the rest of the wall. Example: 25 Talbot Street, Jarvis	
Rose Window: a circular window with ornamental tracery radiating from the centre. Example: Knox Church, Jarvis	
Vergeboard and Finial: also called bargeboards – hang from the projecting end of a roof and are often elaborately carved and ornamented. **Finial:** ornament added to the top of a gable, pinnacle, canopy or spire – a Gothic element. Example: 15 Talbot Street, Jarvis	
Window Hood: A **hood** is the piece found above window openings, usually of an ornate design, and covers the top third of the opening. Hoods are commonly placed above arched or curved openings on both windows and doors. Example: 21 Talbot Street, Jarvis	

Jarvis and Port Dover Building Styles

Gothic Revival, 1830-1890 – These decorative buildings have sharply-pitched gables with highly detailed vergeboards, pointed-arch window openings, and dichromatic brickwork. It is a common style in Ontario. Example: 2145 Main Street, Jarvis	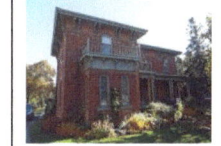
Italianate, 1850-1900 – It has wide-bracketed eaves, belvederes, wrap-around verandahs. Example: 2086 Main Street, Jarvis	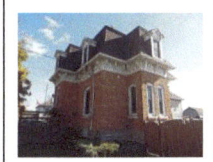
Second Empire, 1860-1880 – The mansard roof is the most noteworthy feature of this style and is evidence of the French origins. Projecting central towers and one or two-storey bays can also be present. Example: 45 Talbot Street, Jarvis	

www.ingramcontent.com/pod-product-compliance
Lightning Source LLC
Chambersburg PA
CBHW040921180526
45159CB00002BA/554